Cambridge Elements ≡

Elements in Music and Musicians 1750–1850
edited by
Simon P. Keefe
University of Sheffield

BACH, HANDEL, AND SCARLATTI

Reception in Britain 1750–1850

Mark Kroll
Boston University

CAMBRIDGE
UNIVERSITY PRESS

CAMBRIDGE
UNIVERSITY PRESS

University Printing House, Cambridge CB2 8BS, United Kingdom

One Liberty Plaza, 20th Floor, New York, NY 10006, USA

477 Williamstown Road, Port Melbourne, VIC 3207, Australia

314–321, 3rd Floor, Plot 3, Splendor Forum, Jasola District Centre,
New Delhi – 110025, India

103 Penang Road, #05–06/07, Visioncrest Commercial, Singapore 238467

Cambridge University Press is part of the University of Cambridge.

It furthers the University's mission by disseminating knowledge in the pursuit of
education, learning, and research at the highest international levels of excellence.

www.cambridge.org
Information on this title: www.cambridge.org/9781009009065
DOI: 10.1017/9781009006880

First published 2022

A catalogue record for this publication is available from the British Library.

ISBN 978-1-009-00906-5 Paperback
ISSN 2732-558X (online)
ISSN 2732-5571 (print)

Bach, Handel, and Scarlatti

Reception in Britain 1750–1850

Elements in Music and Musicians 1750–1850

DOI: 10.1017/9781009006880
First published online: September 2022

Mark Kroll
Boston University
Author for correspondence: Mark Kroll, mkroll@bu.edu

Abstract: The music of Johann Sebastian Bach, George Frederic Handel, and Domenico Scarlatti received more performances, publications, and appreciation in Britain between 1750 and 1850 than in any other country during this era. The compositions of these three seminal baroque composers were heard in the numerous public and private concerts that proliferated at this time; edited, arranged, and published for professionals and amateurs; written about by scholars and journalists; and used as teaching pieces and in pedagogical treatises. This Element examines the reception of their music during this dynamic period in British musical history and places the discussion within the context of the artistic, cultural, economic, and political factors that stimulated such passionate interest in "ancient music." It also offers a vivid picture of the aesthetic concerns of those musicians and audiences involved with this repertoire, providing insights that help us better understand our own encounters with music of the past.

Keywords: Music History, Britain, Bach, Handel, Scarlatti

ISBNs: 9781009009065 (PB), 9781009006880 (OC)
ISSNs: 2732-558X (online), 2732-5571 (print)

Contents

1 Introduction

Palestrina was their Homer.[1]

John Marsh (1752–1828), an accomplished gentleman-musician and indefatigable diarist, had a great deal of difficulty finding breakfast on the morning of May 26, 1784. The opening concert of the first Handel Commemoration was being presented that day, and Marsh tells us in his diary that he was so eager to "insure a seat in a good situation for seeing & hearing [he] got up & had my hairdresser at 7," arising early in order to "be at the doors about half an hour before they open'd w'ich they were to be at 9 o'clock tho' the performance was not to begin until 12." The only problem he faced was where to have his morning meal. He first went "to Anderton's to breakfast at ½ past 7," but "found the house fast shut up & not a window open." Equally futile were his attempts to find an open coffee shop "in the Strand," and even at the "Golden Cross Charing Cross from whence coaches were daily going from 4 and 5 in the morning." However, Marsh eventually did have his breakfast at "the coffee house at the entrance of Westminster Hall," half an hour before the doors opened, where he found "coffee, chocolate & tea all ready, with muffins" that would enable him to "keep up [his] attention to the music without flagging." He goes on to describe in detail his exultation at witnessing one of the most significant events in British musical history.[2]

Marsh's excitement at hearing the music of a composer who had died twenty-five years earlier, and the extraordinary efforts he took to do so, tells us a great deal about the reception of the music of Handel at that time. Nor was he alone in his enthusiasm. In 1784, it was shared by over 2,000 members of the audience, including King George III and Queen Charlotte, and more than 500 performers.[3] In point of fact, interest in older music among British

---

[1] Percy Lovell, "'Ancient' Music in Eighteenth-Century England," *Music & Letters*, vol. 60, no. 4 (October 1979), pp. 401–415, here p. 403, citing Charles Burney, *A General History of Music from the Earliest Ages to the Present Period (1789)*, 2 vols., ed. Frank Mercer (New York: Dover Publications, 1957), vol. ii, p. 163. This comment reflects Charles Burney's astute observation that since Homer occupies "the most ample and honourable place" in the history of ancient poetry, it is "Palestrina, the Homer of the most *Ancient Music* that has been preserved, [who] merits all the reverence and attention which it is in a musical historian's power to bestow."

[2] *The John Marsh Journals: The Life and Times of a Gentleman Composer (1752–1828)*, edited, introduced, and annotated by Brian Robins (Stuyvesant, NY: The Pendragon Press, 1998), pp. 316–319.

[3] For another, equally colorful description of the wide range of events during the 1784 Handel Commemoration, this time by a professional oboist who actually played in the "band," see W. T. Parke, *Musical Memoirs; Comprising an Account of the General State of Music in England from the First Commemoration of Handel in 1784, to the Year 1830* (New York: Da Capo Press, 1970), pp. 36–44. Parke confirms the impressive size of the undertaking, the huge orchestra, and the luxurious accommodations for the elite, such as "the splendid box erected for their Majesties . . . seats covered with crimson cloth." He also echoes what Marsh described about

musicians and audiences, which can be traced back to the seventeenth century, had become very intense by the middle of the eighteenth. It would continue to grow for the next one hundred years, so much so that the music of not only Handel but also Domenico Scarlatti and Johann Sebastian Bach received more performances, publications, attention, and appreciation in Britain between 1750 and 1850 than in any other country and assumed a central role in British musical life.

Ludwig Spohr (1784–1859), whose music was well known and admired in Britain throughout the nineteenth century, said as much during his visit to London in 1833, claiming in an interview for *The Atlas* that it was in this British city that one finds "the only concerts in the world . . . limited to the performance of old music."[4] Admittedly, Spohr here was commenting on the works of Handel that he had heard during his visit, but he might have well been referring to the numerous performances of older music by other composers that had become prevalent in programs in Britain during this era.

Despite Spohr's assertion that Britain was alone in presenting such concerts, which he probably made to please his English hosts, programs of old music, or "historical concerts," were not unknown in countries on the Continent by the 1830s. France, for example, could boast of the "concerts historiques" presented by François-Joseph Fétis at the Paris Conservatoire, where he was serving as librarian. The first, on April 8, 1832, featured works by Peri, Caccini, and Monteverdi, progressing to pieces by Méhul, Rossini, and Weber.[5] Fétis was apparently a proponent of early music beyond his own "concerts historiques." For example, he seems to have encouraged the Hummel piano protégé Ferdinand Hiller to play early keyboard repertoire (on the piano) when he lived in Paris, such as a performance of pieces from a "Virginalbook" on

---

the timing and crush of people at the doors, including a confirmation of Marsh's account about trying to get a good seat when the doors opened at 9 a.m., writing: "the curiosity of the public was so great, that although the performance was not to commence till twelve o'clock, the doors were besieged by nine."

[4] *The Atlas*, August 11, 1833, no. 378, p. 517. As an indication of Spohr's popularity with British audiences and musicians, 228 of his works were performed by the Royal Philharmonic Society on 130 subscription concerts between 1820 and 1896, more than almost any other composer.

[5] See Harry Haskell, *The Early Music Revival: A History* (London: Thames & Hudson, 1988), p. 19. Haskell tells us that "the audience was so enthused" by the program and performances at the second concert in December "that it demanded five encores – after sitting through no less than four hours of sixteenth-century vocal and instrumental music interspersed with Fétis's learned discourse." For further information about Fétis and his "concerts historiques," see Robert Wangermée, *François-Joseph Fétis: musicologue et compositeur* (Bruxelles: Palais des Académies, 1951); Robert Wangermée, "Les techniques de la virtuosité pianistique selon Fétis," *Revue belge de Musicologie*, vol. 26 (1972–1973), pp. 90–105; and Robert Wangermée, "Les Premiers Concerts Historiques à Paris," in *Mélanges Ernest Closson* (Brussels: Societé belge de musicologie, 1948), pp. 185–196, here p. 188.

a concert of April 15, 1835.[6] Hiller would perform at least one unidentified Bach violin sonata with Pierre Baillot (1771–1842) in Paris while living there in the 1830s, and again, probably due to Fétis' influence, played an "Allegro" from a "*Concerto pour 3 pianos*" of J. S. Bach (BWV 1063?) on March 23, 1833, repeating it on December 15 of that year, his fellow pianists being none other than Chopin and Liszt.[7]

Historical concerts were also being presented in Germany around this time.[8] For example, on April 4, 1835, the music association Euterpe sponsored a *historische Konzert* in the Leipzig Hotel de Pologne, titled "Characteristics of German Eighteenth-Century Composers." The early music on the program included an "overture" by Bach [the *Overture in D Major*, BWV 1068?] and the "Hallelujah Chorus" from *Messiah*, along with an overture by Gluck, a chorus from Haydn's *Creation*, the overture to *Die Zauberflöte* by Mozart, and Beethoven's *Symphony No. 7*.[9] Felix Mendelssohn's musical historicism is well known, and will be further discussed in the sections on Handel and Bach.[10] To cite one example here, Mendelssohn, in his capacity as music director of the *Grosse Concerts* in Leipzig, put on three cycles of *historische Konzerte* in 1838, 1841, and 1847, integrating them into the usual subscription concerts of the Gewandhaus.[11]

Spohr made his own contribution to the field with his *Historische Sinfonie*, op. 116 (1839), which consisted of four movements, each dedicated to a different style and era. The first, "Bach-Händel'sche Periode 1720," begins with a short "Largo Grave" in the French Overture style (see Exx. 1a–e), followed by a longer section marked "Allegro Moderato," (See Exx. 1d-e) its

---

[6] Dieter Gutknecht, "Hiller und die Alte Musik: Die Kölner Erstaufführung der *Matthäus-Passion* 1859 von Johann Sebastian Bach," in Peter Ackermann, Arnold Jacobshagen, Roberto Scoccimarro, Wolfram Steinbeck, Laure Schnapper, *Ferdinand Hiller: Komponist, Interpret, Musikvermittler* (Berlin: Merseburger, 2014), pp. 401–414, here p. 405.

[7] For the Baillot performance, see Gutknecht, "Hiller und die Alte Musik," p. 407. For the Bach concerto, see Malou Haine, "Les concerts communs de Ferdinand Hiller et Franz Liszt à Paris dans les années 1830," in *Ferdinand Hiller: Komponist, Interpret, Musikvermittler*, p. 309–327, here pp. 312 and 326.

[8] Early music was not unknown in Germany before the nineteenth century. Prime examples are the salons of wealthy Jewish families in Berlin, where works by J. S. Bach were frequently performed. For further information, see Rebecca Cypess and Nancy Sinkoff, eds., *Sara Levy's World: Gender, Judaism, and the Bach Tradition in Enlightenment Berlin* (Rochester: University of Rochester Press, 2018).

[9] See Nicole Grimes and Angela R. Mace, eds., *Mendelssohn Perspectives* (Surrey: Ashgate, 2012), p. 148.

[10] One of the best sources of information about this aspect of Mendelssohn's activities is Susanna Großmann-Vendrey, *Felix Mendelssohn Bartholdy und die Musik der Vergangenheit* (Regensburg: Gustav Bosse Verlag, 1969), pp. 159–169.

[11] Grimes and Mace, *Mendelssohn Perspectives*, pp. 146–148. Mendelssohn also played Bach violin sonatas with Pierre Baillot in Paris between 1831 and 1832. See Grimes and Mace, *Mendelssohn Perspectives*, p. 320.

Example 1a–c Ludwig Spohr, *Symphony No. 6*, op. 116, "Historische," Movement I, "Bach-Händel'sche Periode 1720," mm. 1–6 (wind parts omitted)

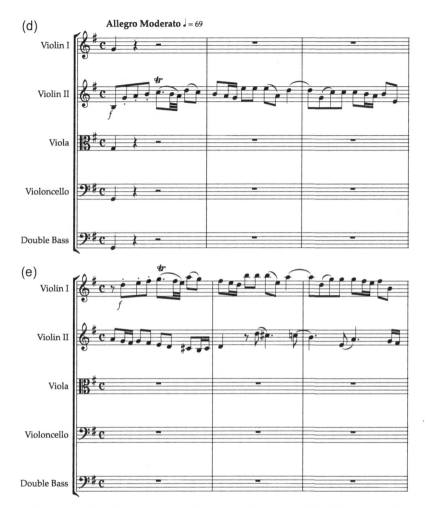

Example 1d–e Ludwig Spohr, *Symphony No. 6*, op. 116, "Historische," Movement I, "Bach-Händel'sche Periode 1720," mm. 8–13 (wind parts omitted)

opening similar to the theme of Bach's "Fugue in C Major" from *The Well-Tempered Clavier*, Book I. After this section comes a homophonic "Pastorale" in the style of Handel, the movement concluding with the fugal material, marked "Tempo primo."

The second movement, titled "Haydn-Mozart'sche Periode 1780," is in that style; the third, "Beethoven'sche Periode 1810," evokes a scherzo by Beethoven; and the last, "Allerneuste Periode 1840," satirized what Haskell describes as "the contemporary idiom that Spohr deplored."[12]

---

[12] Haskell, *The Early Music Revival*, p. 21.

Nevertheless, Spohr's claim in *The Atlas* about London's role as a leader in early-music performance was essentially correct and extended to the rest of the country as well. By the 1830s, and for many years prior to that, Britain was second to none in its commitment to this repertoire, and particularly to works by three of the most important musicians of the Baroque era, who also happened to share the birth year of 1685: D. Scarlatti (d. 1757), G. F. Handel (d. 1759), and J. S. Bach (d. 1750). This Element explores the enthusiastic reception of the music of these three composers in Great Britain between 1750 and 1850, and the artistic, cultural, economic, and political factors that encouraged it, or at least made it possible.

Many of these forces would change, of course, or assume varying degrees of importance and influence over a period of one hundred years, but two that remained constant were money and power. As Nicholas Temperley explains, Britain, and London in particular, became the dominant political and economic force in Europe between 1750 and 1850, as well as the most cosmopolitan, its "lead over all others in wealth and population" translating into musical preeminence as well. This meant more public concerts, more students, and a wider dissemination of all kinds of repertoire because of the city's and the country's global leadership "in the publication of sheet music."[13] The British emphasis on personal freedom and independence, or at least the opportunity to seek it, and the limited state control of cultural institutions also created an atmosphere that encouraged individual entrepreneurship, a valuable advantage for musicians trying to make their way in the world. Such conditions were not easily found on the Continent, if at all, with life in most European nation-states more stringently controlled and proscribed by the upper classes and nobility.

However, it was the British aristocracy, with its complicated social hierarchy and restrictive set of class distinctions, that took the lead in creating the situation that Spohr so admired. For example, the 1784 Handel Commemoration with which we began this section was organized and sponsored by the Concert of Ancient Music, founded in 1776 by a group of "proudly backward-looking" noblemen, as William Weber describes, for the express purpose of performing and listening to early music.[14] Although the Commemoration was open to the general public, the programs of the Concert of Ancient Music were typically limited to fellow nobles and other members of the social elite. Its repertoire was equally rarefied, consisting of works from the beginning of the eighteenth century but also reaching back into the Elizabethan era. Yet nothing like it, in

---

[13] Nicholas Temperley, "London and the Piano, 1760–1860," *The Musical Times*, vol. 129, no. 1744 (June 1988), pp. 289–293, here p. 289.

[14] William Weber, *The Rise of Musical Classics in Eighteenth-Century England: A Study in Canon, Ritual, and Ideology* (Oxford: Clarendon Press, 1992), p. 2.

terms of the scope and number of its concerts, existed outside of Britain, and it is safe to say that it was because of the nobles' efforts that early music in Britain "now rivalled the modern; old works had acquired a certain chic."[15]

Early music also found a natural ally in the religious institutions of Britain, foremost among them the Anglican Church, with its rich musical traditions dating back centuries. A leading figure in this regard was William Boyce, whose monumental publication, *Cathedral Music*, would play a motivating role in the Anglican choral revival.[16] The musicians of the Chapel Royal were also active participants in and proponents of the early music revival. Being able to function equally well in the different worlds of the court, the church, and secular London, they brought, as Weber describes, "a strong professional tradition, and the historical consciousness that went along with it" to foster "new social bases for repertories of old music."[17] A parallel development, the so-called Gothic Revival in religion, included a return to traditional Anglican and Catholic rituals and practices, such as the reinstatement of unaccompanied plainchant. The Gothic Revival would find its way into architecture as well. One such revivalist was Augustus Welby Northmore Pugin (1812–1852). The son of a French émigré who had settled in London in 1792, he acquired a considerable reputation, both as a draftsman and as an editor of illustrated books on Gothic architecture, becoming a fervent advocate for the revival of this style of architecture for both secular and sacred spaces, claiming that it was ideal for England and perfectly "suited to our country and climate."[18] Pugin was not shy about his opinions. On one occasion, he even castigated his fellow architects in 1850 for designing churches "whose appearance is something between a dancing-room and a mechanic's institute."[19]

The role of the royal family was also significant, as evidenced by the enthusiastic support for the 1784 commemoration of King George III. His motivations, however, were perhaps more political than musical. For him the 1784 Commemoration was not merely a series of performances of music by his

---

[15] Weber, *The Rise of Musical Classics*, p. 2.

[16] The *Cathedral Music* was published in 1760, 1768, 1773, and 1788, and enlarged by Samuel Arnold in 1790. See Lovell, "Ancient Music in Eighteenth-Century England," p. 407. Another example is John Page's *Harmonia Sacra, a Collection of Anthems in Score, Selected . . . from the most Eminent Masters of the Sixteenth, Seventeenth, and Eighteenth Centuries*. See Peter Holman, *Life after Death: The Viola da Gamba in Britain from Purcell to Dolmetsch* (Woodbridge: The Boydell Press, 2010), p. 303.

[17] Weber, *The Rise of Musical Classics*, p. 9.

[18] George Germann, *Gothic Revival in Europe and Britain: Sources, Influences and Ideas* (London: Lund Humphries with the Architectural Association, 1972), pp. 69–73, here p. 70, citing A[ugustus] Welby [Northmore] Pugin, *A Letter to A. W. Hakewill, Architect, in Answer to His "Reflections on the Style for Rebuilding the Houses of Parliament"* (Salisbury, 1835), p. 13.

[19] Cited in Haskell, *The Early Music Revival*, p. 18.

favorite composer. It was an irresistible opportunity to put royal power and prerogative, not to mention royal musical sophistication, on full display before an audience of thousands of his subjects, in no less a venue than Westminster Abbey, itself a symbol of royal continuity. It also came at a propitious time, when the king was dealing with a variety of political problems, such as the fallout and angst caused by the American Revolution (i.e., the recent loss of the American colonies); a constitutional crisis between the Crown and the Parliament; a difficult election that year; and the unification of "Tory and Whig parties within a new political community."[20]

As we shall examine in the remaining sections of this Element, the royal family's advocacy for early music would remain strong through the end of Queen Victoria's reign, thanks in great part to the influence of Prince Albert. The Queen, however, reportedly found most of this repertoire boring, with the exception of Handel, of course.[21] Albert, an avid music lover and skilled amateur musician, even served as the director of the Ancient Concerts from 1840 to 1848 and, starting in 1843, assumed a greater role by choosing the programs. These, as Temperley tells us, could consist of "medieval hymns and chansons, motets and mass movements by Palestrina, a concerto by Cavalieri (played on viols), arias by Cesti and Stradella, fugues and choruses by Bach," in addition to music by Handel, Haydn, Mozart, Beethoven, Gluck, and even "curiosities like Rousseau's *Le Devin du Village*."[22] Notably, the Queen's subscriptions to the Breitkopf complete editions of Handel and Bach, which were most likely initiated by the Prince Consort, were kept up by Victoria, or a member of her staff, after Albert's death until the editions were complete.

Equally important were influences outside of religious, aristocratic, or royal spheres. These included intellectual and aesthetic movements, such as Romantic antiquarianism. For example, William Shield (1748–1829) and his friend, the folk-song collector Joseph Ritson (1752–1803), collaborated to publish *A Select Collection of English Songs* in 1783, and somewhat later another avid collector and advocate, Stafford Smith (1750–1836), used a large selection from the *Mulliner Book*, which he owned at that time, in *Musica Antiqua* (published in 1812).[23]

---

[20] Weber, *The Rise of Musical Classics*, p. 225.

[21] See Nicholas Temperley, "The Prince Consort, Champion of Music," *The Musical Times*, vol. 102, no. 1426 (December 1961), pp. 762–764, here p. 763. Temperly adds: "At two concerts given by her at Buckingham Palace in 1839, every single item on the programme was a vocal extract from an Italian opera, with a heavy preponderance of Rossini and Donizetti. All were sung by Italians, accompanied at the piano by Costa."

[22] See Temperley, "The Prince Consort, Champion of Music," p. 763.

[23] Cited in Holman, *Life after Death*, pp. 305–306. See also Wendy Heller, *Music in the Baroque* (New York: W. W. Norton, 2013), pp. 46–49.

Antiquarianism was also featured in literary movements, such as the Gothic novel, as represented by a host of writers, including Horace Walpole (e.g., *The Castle of Otranto*), Ann Radcliffe (e.g., *The Mysteries of Udolpho*), Frances Burney, Mary Hays, William Godwin, Mary Wollstonecraft, and Sir Walter Scott, who often satirized some of the excesses of both the Gothic novel and Romantic antiquarianism.[24] The influence of historicism that created such a strong interest in early-music performance was also felt in other humanistic disciplines, including painting, sculpture, and scholarship. For example, when the "Elgin Marbles" that Lord Elgin had stolen from the Parthenon in Athens were displayed in London in 1807, the response was "electric" among both the public and British painters and sculptors as well.[25] The same could be said of the nascent discipline of musicology. It is no surprise that it is in Britain that we find the first full-length biography of a composer (John Mainwaring's *Memoirs of the Life of the Late George Frederic Handel*, 1760); the first "musicological" histories (e.g., by Hawkins and Burney); and the first collected edition of a single composer (Arnold's *The Works of Handel*, 1787–1797).[26]

The performances of the music of D. Scarlatti, Handel, and J. S. Bach also received impetus from Britain's academic institutions, such as Oxford University, a topic to which we will return in later sections, and from numerous private or semi-aristocratic organizations formed to support the cause of early music. In addition to the previously mentioned Concert of Ancient Music, the period after 1750 witnessed the formation of many important musical organizations, including the "Sons of the Clergy," "Madrigal Society," "Catch Club," "Glee Club," "Concentores Sodales," and "Motett Society."[27]

Britain's vibrant music publishing industry, which can trace its roots to the pioneering work of John Playford and others in seventeenth-century London, was greatly expanded by a new generation of music publishers that appeared after 1800, chief among them Samuel Chappell, Vincent Novello, and Thomas Boosey. They issued numerous high-quality editions of large swatches of this

---

[24] See Michael Gamer, *Romanticism and the Gothic: Genre, Reception, and Canon Formation* (Cambridge: Cambridge University Press, 2004), and Carol Margaret Davison, *Gothic Literature, 1764–1824* (Cardiff: University of Wales Press, 2009).

[25] Derek Carew, *The Mechanical Muse: The Pianos, Pianism and Piano Music, c. 1760–1850* (Aldershot: Ashgate, 2007), p. 169.

[26] Holman, *Life after Death*, p. 305.

[27] The Concert of Ancient Music was initially founded as the Academy of Vocal Music in 1726 and then became the Academy of Ancient Music, presenting a series of biweekly semiprivate concerts of old music from 1733 until its demise in 1796. See Philip Olleson and Fiona M. Palmer, "Publishing Music from the Fitzwilliam Museum, Cambridge: The Work of Vincent Novello and Samuel Wesley in the 1820s," *Journal of the Royal Musical Association*, vol. 130, no. 1 (2005), pp. 38–73, here pp. 41–42. See also Haskell, *The Early Music Revival*, p. 18; and Holman, *Life after Death*, pp. 303–304.

early repertoire, while at the same time producing volumes geared to the mass market, such as arrangements of large scores and easy piano versions of popular arias and songs. These were not only profitable, but served an educational purpose, making early music available to a large and enthusiastic market that wanted not only to hear and study these works, but also to play or sing them.[28]

Money, as noted at the beginning of this section, was one of the major factors that made Britain, and especially London, a center for early-music performance between 1750 and 1850. Indeed, its outsize share of the world's wealth during this era enabled it to support a wide range of institutions, businesses, and individual citizens dedicated to the pursuit of this repertoire. Britain also attracted an influx of foreign musicians, who came from almost every country or region in Europe – Italy, Germany, Bohemia, Austria, and to a lesser degree, France and Spain – for a variety of reasons, but primarily to take advantage of the financial opportunities they could not find in their home countries. Leopold Mozart acknowledged this in a letter of 1754, writing that London was a good place "to haul in a good catch of guineas."[29] Some came to visit, others to settle permanently. August Wendborn (1742–1811) wrote about those who came only for a temporary stay: "Many foreign singers, fiddlers, and dancers, are extravagantly paid; and, if they are the least frugal, they are enabled to retire to their own country, where they may live in affluence, enriched by English money."[30] The same was true for Johann Nepomuk Hummel almost fifty years later. After returning home to Weimar in 1830 from one of his successful (and profitable) tours to Britain, he was probably not surprised to receive a letter from his friend Adolphe Wiele on August 20 of that year that did not dwell on the artistic merits of the tour, but rather asked: "How did it go? Did the Guineas perform well and turn out in great numbers?"[31]

While there might have been an occasional grumble by British musicians who felt eclipsed by their foreign counterparts, on the whole these musical émigrés, whether visiting for a short time or settling permanently, gave back to the host country as much as they received. The Italians received an early and

---

[28] See Colin Timothy Eatcock, *Mendelssohn and Victorian England* (Surrey: Ashgate, 2009), p. 14.

[29] Leopold Mozart, Chelsea, to Lorenz Hagenauer, Salzburg, September 13, 1764, in Emily Anderson, ed., *The Letters of Mozart and his Family*, 3rd ed., S. Sadie and F. Smart (rev.) (London: Macmillan, 1990), p. 52.

[30] Gebhardt Friedrich August Wendborn, *Die Zustand des Staats, der religion, der Gelehrsamkeit und die Kunst in Grosbritannien gegen das Ende des achtzehnten Jahrhunderts*, 4 vols., Berlin, 1785–1788, translated by the author, *A View of England towards the Close of the Eighteenth Century*, 2 vols. (London: G. G. J. and J. Robinson, 1791), vol. 2, p. 237.

[31] Details of Hummel's tours to Britain can be found in Mark Kroll, *Johann Nepomuk Hummel: A Musician's Life and World* (Lanham, MD: Scarecrow Press, 2007), pp. 102–103, 127–135, and 136–150. For the Wiele letter, see Kroll, *Johann Nepomuk Hummel*, p. 135.

particularly warm welcome, especially after the English publications in 1692 of Arcangelo Corelli's *Sonatas for Violin and Basso Continuo*, op. 1, and later his *Concerti Grossi*, op. 5 [1714], which, according to Roger North in 1728, "cleared ye ground of all other sorts of musick whatsoever ... and became to ye musitians like ye bread of life."[32] Corelli's music not only became the daily bread of British musicians and audiences, but also increased the demand for the service of countless other Italian violinist-composers, many of whom streamed across the English channel on the coattails of their illustrious Roman countryman.[33] The long list includes Francesco Veracini, Pietro Castrucci, Francesco Geminiani, Felice Giardini, and many others.[34] Muzio Clementi (1752–1832), a later Italian immigrant, would play an important and, in fact, central role in the popularity and appreciation of the music of D. Scarlatti, Handel, and J. S. Bach during the late eighteenth and early nineteenth centuries. His contributions will be discussed in detail throughout the following sections.

Composers and performers from Germany, Austria, and other German-speaking lands would also enrich the musical life of Britain in numerous ways. One notable example, Johann (John) Christopher Pepusch (1667–1752), who was born in Berlin but moved to Great Britain circa 1700, exerted a major influence in inspiring interest in early music among his adopted countrymen, especially with the part he played in establishing the Academy of Ancient Music in 1726, an organization he faithfully served until his death.[35]

---

[32] Roger North, *The Musicall Gramarian*, ed. Hilda Andrews (London, 1925), p. 37. Cited in Norris Lynn Stephens, "Charles Avison: An Eighteenth-Century English Composer, Musician and Writer" (Ph.D. diss., University of Pittsburgh, 1968), p. 93.

[33] It is interesting to note that Corelli's influence, or at least that of his music, had not greatly diminished at the end of the eighteenth century, as Charles Burney described in 1789: "The *Concertos* of Corelli seem to have withstood all the attacks of time and fashion ... they preclude criticism and make us forget that there is any other Music of the same kind existing." Burney, *A General History of Music*, p. 442.

[34] Many violinists were also opera-orchestra leaders (Castrucci, Carbonelli, Veracini, Giardini, Celestino, Pugnani, Thomas Pinto, and Viotti). Others were tutti players, like Luigi Borghi, Salpietro, and Soderini. City musical societies were sometimes led by Italians; Geminiani (Philo-Musicae et Architecturae Societas), Prospero Castrucci (Castle Concert), and Giardini and Chiabrano (King's Arms Concert). Castrucci and Carbonelli led Handel oratorios, and often violinists played concertos between the acts of oratorio seasons. For a full discussion see Simon McVeigh, "Italian Violinists in Eighteenth Century London," in *The Eighteenth-Century Diaspora of Italian Music and Musicians*, ed. Reinhard Strom (Turnhout: Brepols, 2001), pp. 139–176, here pp. 155–156.

[35] Pepusch was helped by his extensive library of works by older composers, and also by his wife, the former opera singer Margarita de l'Epine, who was clearly an accomplished keyboardist as well, since she was able to play Elizabethan virginal music from "Queen Elizabeth's Virginal Book" (now the Fitzwilliam Virginal Book) from her husband's collection. See A. Hyatt King, *Some British Collectors of Music c. 1600–1960* (Cambridge: Cambridge University Press, 1963), p. 31, who wrote: "there seems little doubt that the *primum mobile*, the great impetus to collecting on a large scale and to the related growth of musical scholarship, came from Pepusch." Cited in Lovell, "'Ancient' Music in Eighteenth-Century England," pp. 408–409.

The most famous German émigré of the first half of the seventeenth century is, of course, Handel, who came to London from Halle and Hanover via Italy.

Heading the list of the next generation of German musicians are Johann Christian Bach and Carl Friedrich Abel. Both established residence in London (Abel in 1758 or 1759, J. C. Bach in 1762), where they founded the popular and justly admired "Bach-Abel" concerts, and even lived together for a period of time. Some specific contributions of J. C. Bach, who served as music master to Queen Charlotte from 1763 until his death in 1782, will be discussed in the section on J. S. Bach. The German-speaking émigrés and/or visitors who followed J. C. Bach and Abel played an especially crucial role in the introduction of the music of J. S. Bach into the British musical canon, their work culminating with the advocacy of Felix Mendelssohn and Ignaz Moscheles.

Thus, due to the wide array of factors, influences, and confluence of events, as well as the efforts of a dedicated group of musicians, critics, teachers, and other supporters, the ground was indeed cleared for early music to flourish in Britain during the eighteenth and nineteenth centuries. This was particularly true for D. Scarlatti, G. F. Handel, and J. S. Bach, and it is to these masters that we now turn our attention.

2 Domenico Scarlatti

"Domenico Scarlatti may justly be ranked among the great masters of this age." Charles Avison (1709–80), of Newcastle, England, wrote these words of praise for Scarlatti in 1753, in his *Essay on Musical Expression*.[36] Avison also singled out Scarlatti a decade later, in 1764, extolling the "*peculiar* Beauties" of his sonatas and the "*fine Fancy* of the Italian."[37] Avison's unequivocal and lifelong

---

[36] Charles Avison, *An Essay on Musical Expression . . . The Second Edition, with Alterations and Large Additions*, (London: C. Davis, 1753; facs. New York: Broude Brothers, 1967), p. 52, footnote. See Mark Kroll, "*Con Furia*: Charles Avison and the Scarlatti Sect in Eighteenth-Century England," in *The Early Keyboard Sonata in Italy and Beyond* (Turnhout: Brepols, 2016), pp. 252–277.

[37] Charles Avison, preface to his *Six Sonatas for the Harpsichord with Accompanyments for Two Violins and Violoncello*. Avison praises two other foreign musicians in this preface – J. P. Rameau and C. P. E. Bach – writing: "Among the various Productions of foreign Composers for the Harpsichord, the Sonatas of SCARLATTI, RAMEAU AND CARLO-BACH have their *peculiar* Beauties. The *fine Fancy* of the Italian – the *spirited Science* of the Frenchman – and the German's *diffusive Expression* are the distinguishing Signatures of their Music." The absence of praise for Handel is not unexpected. Avison was often critical of several aspects of Handel's compositional style, inspiring the wrath of many devoted Handelians, the Oxford professor William Hayes in particular.

admiration for this virtuoso composer of harpsichord sonatas and his admittedly idiosyncratic musical style is notable for a number of reasons. For one thing, Avison was not an Italian émigré like his teacher and mentor Geminiani or, somewhat later, Clementi, eager to promote and carry on the legacy of Corelli and his fellow countrymen, but a native-born British subject who spent almost his entire life and career in Newcastle in the north of England. Avison, moreover, was not even primarily a harpsichordist, but rather a conductor and a prolific composer of Italian-style concerti grossi.[38]

What is more relevant to this discussion is the fact that Avison's comment comes at the very beginning of the era to which this Element is dedicated, underscoring the fact that it was not Handel, already a living icon in his adopted country with a substantial reputation abroad, who was the first to attract the attention and dedication of British revivalists. Nor was it J. S. Bach, who was recognized as a master in parts of Germany but was scarcely known in Great Britain at this time. Rather, the honor goes to Domenico Scarlatti, an Italian who spent most of his life in relative obscurity in Portugal and Spain.

The initial impetus for Scarlatti achieving this status preceded Avison by more than a decade, however, beginning in 1739, and came from a group of English musicians with an almost fanatical devotion to the music of Domenico Scarlatti. Dubbed by Charles Burney "the Scarlatti sect," its most prominent members were Joseph Kelway (ca. 1702–82) and Thomas Roseingrave (1690/1–1766).[39] Burney described Kelway as a brilliant harpsichordist who "kept Scarlatti's best Lessons in constant practice [and] executed the most difficult lessons of Scarlatti, in a manner peculiarly neat and delicate."[40] Roseingrave's most significant contribution was his collection of forty-two Scarlatti sonatas that he published in 1739 as *XLII Suites de Pieces Pour le Clavecin: En deux*

---

[38] For further information on Avison's life and works, see Jenny Burchell, *Polite or Commercial Concerts?* (New York: Garland, 1996); *Music in the British Provinces, 1690–1914*, edited by Rachel Cowgill and Peter Holman (Aldershot: Ashgate, 2007); *Charles Avison's Essay on Musical Expression*, edited by Pierre Dubois, (Aldershot: Ashgate, 2004); P. M. Horsley, "Charles Avison: The Man and His Milieu," in *Music & Letters*, vol. 55, no. 1 (January 1974), pp. 5–23; *Concerto-Grosso Arrangements of Francesco Geminiani's Sonatas for Violin and Basso Continuo, Op. 1, Nos. 1–10 and 12*, edited by Mark Kroll (Middleton, WI: A-R Editions, 2010); Roz Southey, *Music-Making in North-East England during the Eighteenth Century* (Aldershot: Ashgate, 2006); and Roz Southey, Margaret Maddison, and David Hughes, *The Ingenious Mr Avison* (Newcastle: Tyne Bridge Publishing, 2009).

[39] Charles Burney, *A General History*, vol. II, p. 1009. The English furor over the Scarlatti sonatas has been well documented. See Richard Newton, "The English Cult of Domenico Scarlatti," *Music & Letters*, vol. 20, no. 2 (April 1939), pp. 138–156.

[40] Burney, *A General History*, vol. 2, p. 1009. Kelway was organist at the church of St. Martin-in-the-Fields, and from 1764, harpsichord master to Queen Charlotte. For more information on Kelway, see Malcolm Boyd, *Domenico Scarlatti – Master of Music* (New York: Schirmer Books, 1986), pp. 213–215 and 226, and Ralph Kirkpatrick, *Domenico Scarlatti* (Princeton, NJ: Princeton University Press, 1983), p. 125.

Volumes, shortly after the London publication of Scarlatti's *Essercizi per Gravicembalo* during the same year.[41] It is interesting but not surprising that among the subscribers to Roseingrave's publication can be found the names of several of the people who figure prominently in our discussion of the growth of early music in Britain, such as Thomas Arne, John Pepusch, Francesco Geminiani, William Boyce, and of course, Charles Avison.[42] Somewhat later, John Worgan (1724–90), a student of Roseingrave who served as organist at the Vauxhall pleasure gardens from 1751 to 1759 (he became composer in residence in 1753) and then again in 1770–4, would join this group of Scarlatti aficionados; according to Burney, Worgan "became a great collector of [Scarlatti's] pieces, some of which he had been honoured with from Madrid by the author himself."[43]

It should also be underscored that Avison, although a sufficiently skilled harpsichordist and organist for his purposes, was not a keyboard player by profession like Roseingrave, Kelway, or Worgan. He therefore turned to the genre to which he devoted almost all of his compositional career – the concerto grosso – to promote and perform Scarlatti's music, and it was through Avison's concerto transcriptions that Scarlatti's music became best known in the British Isles after 1750.[44] This was certainly true for John Marsh, who documents in his diaries on numerous occasions that he was quite familiar with Avison's "Scarlatti" concerti, but fails to mention the harpsichord originals. For example, Marsh writes on November 16, 1781: "I play'd a concerto of Avison's made from one of Scarlatti's lessons."[45] He tells us on 29 December 1786 that he "played Avison Scarlatti's Concerto" (the program also included Marsh's own "Rondeau of Largo Lee"), and an entry from March 22, 1787 records another performance of an "Avison Scarlatti's

---

[41] For additional information about the *Essercizi*, which contained sonatas K. 1–30 and were published between April 21, 1738 and January 31, 1739, see Boyd, *Scarlatti*, pp. 139–140, 157–159, and 402, and Kirkpatrick, *Domenico Scarlatti*, pp. 101–104 and 156–161.

[42] Some other subscribers to Roseingrave's edition include William de Fesch, Morris Green, Edward Purcell, and Joseph Mahoon ("Harpsichord Maker to His Majesty"). Boyce also owned a copy of the *Essercizi*, as well as music by Abel, Avison, Byrd, Cavalli, Croft, D'Anglebert, Dowland, Frescobaldi, Fux, Geminiani, Graun, Lassus, Lully, Purcell, and Alessandro Scarlatti. See Robert J. Bruce and H. Diack Johnstone, "A Catalogue of the Truly Valuable and Curious Library of Music in the Possession of Dr. William Boyce (1779)," in *Royal Music Association Research Chronicle*, no. 43 (2010), pp. 111–171.

[43] Burney, *A General History*, vol. 2, p. 1009. According to Burney in his Scarlatti article in Rees' *The Cyclopedia*, "Worgan played no other music, except his own. In short, everyone played or tried to play, Scarlatti's." See Boyd, *Domenico Scarlatti*, p. 213. John was the brother of James Worgan (1715–53), who served as organist at Vauxhall from 1737 to 1751.

[44] Avison went much further than transcription and essentially rewrote many of the Scarlatti sonatas he used. For a description and analysis of this practice and technique, see Kroll, "*Con Furia*: Charles Avison and the Scarlatti Sect in Eighteenth-Century England," pp. 260–274.

[45] *The John Marsh Journals*, p. 253.

Concerto," this time in Canterbury.[46] On February 13, 1789, Marsh again performed an unnamed arrangement of a Scarlatti sonata by Avison, while also having the opportunity to hear his "new Symphony in B-flat [which he] had worked hard at to get finish'd in time & w'ch went off very well"; and he was still playing Avison's Scarlatti concerti on September 8, 1796.[47] What is particularly striking is that Marsh never once mentions hearing or playing a Scarlatti sonata on the harpsichord, over a period of many decades, confirming that his knowledge of this music, as it was for most of his British contemporaries at this time, typically came from the Avison concerti.

One contemporary of Marsh, however, Ambrose Pittman, did know Scarlatti's keyboard sonatas in the original versions, but seems to have had some serious reservations about them. Pittman, reportedly a student of Thomas Arne, was not a gentleman-amateur like Marsh, but a professional keyboard teacher. Around 1780 he published fifteen sonatas from Roseingrave's 1739 volumes as *The Beauties of Domenico Scarlatti: Selected from His Suites de Lecons ... and Revised with a Variety of Improvements by Ambrose Pitman.*[48] Pittman was hardly a member of a "Scarlatti sect" dedicated to the faithful promotion of the composer. Nor did he follow Avison's lead by honoring the composer with some inspired arrangements for string ensemble. Rather, Pittman was apparently so uncomfortable with several features of Scarlatti's originals that he set out to "improve" them, essentially by trying to make them easier to read and play. He describes his intentions and methods in the preface, writing that because the reception of Scarlatti's sonatas has "been greatly retarded by the many superfluous and studied difficulties with which they abound," he chose "to remove these Obstacles, which have, in some measure, obscured such admirable Lessons from Public Notice, and that they may, in future, be more readily understood by the Student." This included divesting "them of their pedantic difficulties" by replacing "the Tenor Cleff, intended only to perplex the Sight of the Performer," with "that of the Treble, as being more familiar to the generality of Practitioners," and avoiding or changing "unnatural and cramp positions of the hands [so] that the fingering might be rendered easy and graceful."

Pittman, however, did much more to the Scarlatti originals than just divest "them of their pedantic difficulties." He made substantial changes to the musical text that eliminated some of the features that made Scarlatti's harpsichord sonatas unique masterpieces of the genre. This can be seen by

---

[46] *The John Marsh Journals*, pp. 393 and 397, respectively.

[47] *The John Marsh Journals*, pp. 447 and 595, respectively.

[48] All the sonatas were taken from the Roseingrave edition. There is no publication date, but it probably appeared in the mid 1780s.

Example 2 Domenico Scarlatti, *Sonata in D Major*, K. 29, mm. 16–19

comparing Scarlatti's *Sonata in D Major*, K. 29 with Pittman's version, titled "Lesson IV." For example, he changes the tempo "Presto" of the original sonata to "Brillante," adds trills and removes voices (see Exx. 2 and 3), recomposes the musical text (see Exx. 4 and 5), omits some of Scarlatti's trademark dissonances (see Exx. 6 and 7), and not only rewrites the conclusion but adds measures to it (see Exx. 8 and 9).

Thus, it seems that the harpsichord sonatas of Domenico Scarlatti were not ideally served in Britain during the forty years following the groundbreaking work of Roseingrave, Kelway, and Worgan in the middle of the eighteenth century. Rather than hearing these brilliant keyboard works in their original form, the majority of British musicians and audiences experienced them either through a string arrangement, as excellent as Avison's might be, or in questionable versions from Pittman's edition. Fortunately, this situation was remedied, quite appropriately, by a fellow Italian, the émigré Muzio Clementi. A brilliant keyboard player and a highly sophisticated musician, Clementi probably did more to promote the music of Scarlatti than any other person in Britain.

According to various reports, especially that of J. A. Méreaux (1802–74), a Parisian who seems to have had at least one lesson with Clementi in 1820, and who himself published twenty Scarlatti sonatas in the second volume of his comprehensive keyboard collection, *Les Clavecinistes de 1637 à 1790*, Clementi "practiced and studied continuously" Scarlatti sonatas, as well as music by J. S. Bach, C. P. E. Bach, and Handel, when he was in residence at the home of Sir Peter Beckford (1740–1811) between approximately 1766/7 and 1774.[49]

---

[49] The definitive biography of Clementi is by Leon Plantinga, *Clementi: His Life and Music* (London: Oxford University Press, 1977). For a discussion of Clementi's residence at the

Example 3 Ambrose Pittman, Lesson IV, mm. 16–19

Example 4 Domenico Scarlatti, *Sonata in D Major*, K. 29, mm. 47–49

Example 5 Ambrose Pittman, Lesson IV, mm. 47–49

Example 6 Domenico Scarlatti, *Sonata in D Major*, K. 29, mm. 70–71

Beckford estate, see Plantinga, *Clementi: His Life and Music*, pp. 1–8. For his admiration of Scarlatti, see Plantinga, *Clementi: His Life and Music*, pp. 49 and 140–142, among other sections in the book. A complete publication of Mereaux's *Les Clavecinistes*, which contains his description of Clementi's practice habits, was brought out by Heugel & Cie. in 1867.

Example 7 Ambrose Pittman, Lesson IV, mm. 71–72

Example 8 Domenico Scarlatti, *Sonata in D Major*, K. 29, mm. 84–87

Example 9 Ambrose Pittman, Lesson IV, mm. 87–91

Clementi's first public performances of Scarlatti's music can be traced to his visit to Paris in 1780–1 (or possibly later, ca. 1783–4), when he played Scarlatti's *Sonata in A Major*, K. 113, presumably on the piano.[50] By October 1784, during

---

[50] See Plantinga, *Clementi: His Life and Music*, chapter III, passim.

his reported sojourn in and near Bern, Clementi's renditions of Scarlatti's music drew praise from a person identified only as "a Schoolmaster."[51]

Not content with merely playing individual sonatas on random occasions, however, and being intimately familiar with a wide range of Scarlatti's works after so many years of study and practice, Clementi brought out one of the most important publications of Scarlatti's sonatas to appear in Britain, his *Scarlatti's Chefs d'Oeuvre, for the Harpsichord or Piano-forte; Selected from an Elegant Collection of Manuscripts, in the Possession of Muzio Clementi.*[52] Published on June 6, 1791, this collection represents the first English edition of the following Scarlatti sonatas:

Clementi no.	*K. (Kirkpatrick no.)*	*Key*	*Source (primary, according to Kirkpatrick)*
1	378	F major [1754?]	Venice VIII, 21
3	380	E major [1754?]	Venice VIII, 23, in F
4	490	D major [1756?]	Venice XII, 7
5	400	D major [1754?]	Venice IX, 13
6	475	Eb major [1756?]	Venice XI, 22
7	381	Eb major [1754?]	Venice VIII, 24, in E
8	206	E major [1753?]	Venice III, 1
9	531	E major [1757?]	Venice XIII, 18
10	462	F minor [1756?]	Venice XI, 9
11	463	F minor [1756?]	Venice XI, 10

---

[51] See Plantinga, *Clementi: His Life and Music*, p. 72, and Stephen Daw, "Muzio Clementi as an Original Advocate, Collector and Performer, in Particular of J. S. Bach and D. Scarlatti," in *Bach, Handel, Scarlatti Tercentenary Essays*, ed. Peter Williams (Cambridge: Cambridge University Press, 1985), pp. 61–74, here p. 62.

[52] See Daw, "Muzio Clementi as an Original Advocate," p. 63. Daw writes that "Shortly after its publication, or simultaneously with it, Pleyel of Paris published his own edition of *Scarlatti's Chefs d'Oeuvre* under the title *Methode Pour la Pianoforte par Muzio Clementi contenant ... Cinquante Lerons doightees par les Compositeurs les plus celebres, tels que Handl* [sic] *... Bach ... Scarlali* [sic] *... &C. Daw,*" "Muzio Clementi as an Original Advocate," p. 64.

The missing number 2 is anonymous, and number 12 in F major is now attributed to Antonio Soler.[53]

More Scarlatti sonatas would be published by Clementi on October 26, 1801, when the first edition of his *Introduction to the Art of Playing on the Piano Forte* was registered at Stationers' Hall. It included the following "Lessons" by Scarlatti: "XV" (*Sonata in D Minor*, K. 34); "XXX MINUETTO" (*Sonata in B-Flat Major*, K. 42), "XXXV Allegro" (*Sonata in G Minor*, K. 35); and "XLIII Minuet" (*Sonata in C Minor*, K. 40). Scarlatti's sonatas, in fact, would appear as "lessons" in every subsequent issue and edition of Clementi's *Introduction* through 1830, plus the Appendices of 1811 and after about 1833.[54] Clementi would also publish two more sonatas of Scarlatti on February 20, 1802, in volume 2 of *Clementi's Selection of Practical Harmony for the Organ or Piano Forte* (Tyson 1967 Wo 7, II). They are listed as "Scarlatti Fuga 1" (i.e., *Sonata in D Minor*, K. 41) and "Scarlatti Fuga 2" (i.e., the *Sonata in G Minor*, K. 30), with the added comment: "The following, by Domenico Scarlatti, is the celebrated CAT'S FUGUE."[55]

Considering Clementi's considerable efforts on behalf of Scarlatti, and the relatively wide dissemination of his sonatas after 1791 through Clementi's publications, one would have expected an equally broad and enthusiastic reception among performers, scholars, and audiences in Britain for decades to come. Unfortunately this was not to be the case. Despite the promising start in the middle of the eighteenth century, including the concertos of Avison, as well as the efforts of Clementi, Domenico Scarlatti did not achieve the same place in the British early-music canon as did the music of Handel and J. S. Bach. In terms of actual public performances, Scarlatti sonatas essentially disappeared from the concert stage during the last half of the eighteenth century and for the first thirty years of the nineteenth, until Ignaz Moscheles, a long-time close friend and colleague of Clementi's, began playing them in London at his historical soirées in 1837.[56]

One of the reasons these sonatas were ignored can be traced to the genre itself. Audiences in Britain had become accustomed to grand performances of Handel oratorios, with the proverbial cast of thousands, and to other large choral works. Operas were also popular, and it should also be remembered that this was the beginning of the symphonic era, when listeners could be attracted by the sounds and colors of orchestral works, such as symphonies by Haydn, Mozart, and, somewhat later, Beethoven. Programs, such as those offered by the Royal

---

[53] Information taken from Daw, "Muzio Clementi as an Original Advocate," p. 63.

[54] For a complete discussion of the history and contents of the *Introduction*, including all editions, issues, appendices, and foreign editions, see Sandra P. Rosenblum, "New Introduction" to the *Introduction to the Art of Playing on the Piano Forte* (New York: Da Capo Press, 1974), pp. v–xxxix.

[55] See Daw, "Muzio Clementi as an Original Advocate," p. 65.

[56] For information on these soirées, see Mark Kroll, *Ignaz Moscheles and the Changing World of Musical Europe* (Woodbridge: The Boydell Press, 2014), pp. 284–297.

Philharmonic, also featured a wide diversity of repertoire and ensembles, ranging from vocal selections to instrumental sonatas and chamber music, to overtures and symphonies. All of this was daunting competition for a single harpsichordist, playing two-voice compositions by an admittedly eccentric composer.

That eccentricity also might have been a factor in the hesitancy to fully embrace Scarlatti. What we now view as the unique and attractive stylistic features of his compositional style – unusual and sometimes quixotic harmonic progressions; crashing dissonances (often unresolved in proper "textbook" fashion); chords of five, six, seven voices, and more, seemingly constructed with pitches from two remote tonalities; colorful keyboard figuration (such as long sections of repeated notes, or skips from one end of the keyboard to another) that seemed more like sound effects than "proper" music; and evocations of folk music or other nontraditional sources – might have been too difficult to be fully understood, or more accurately, accepted, by a large number of listeners, performers, and critics.

It also caused a certain level of discomfort among those at the highest levels of British musical scholarship and criticism – the tastemakers, if you will – who felt that this Scarlatti style seemed to transgress the bounds of good taste and musical propriety, more than anything Handel and J. S. Bach wrote for the keyboard, or what was being composed for the piano during this era. It should be recalled that Scarlatti himself anticipated this reaction when he wrote in the preface to his *Essercizi*: "Whether you be dilettante or Professors, in these compositions do not expect any profound Learning, but rather an ingenious Jesting with Art."[57]

One of those "Professors" turned out to be the Oxford music teacher Sir William Crotch, a passionate advocate for "ancient music" and the creation of a "scholarly canon," who criticized "composers [who] have left violations of these rules in their works" in his essay on correct part writing.[58] He is referring to Scarlatti here, of course, but also mentions other lesser composers who do this "from oversight," excusing Scarlatti as "perhaps the only one who professedly disregarded them for the sake of producing good effects." Crotch also adds, perhaps with a sigh of relief: "But whatever may have been the success of this great master, the passages in which he has transgressed the rules do not appear to have become

[57] English translation in Kirkpatrick, *Domenico Scarlatti*, pp. 101–102. It should also be noted that Scarlatti's rule-breaking approach was inspired by the works of a school of almost anarchic Spanish writers and playwrights he encountered when he moved to the Iberian peninsula, such as those of Friar Benito Jerónimo Feijóo, Lope de Vega, and Pedro Calderón de la Barca, all of whom expressed complete disdain for "learned professors." Cited in James Iffland, "Scarlatti and the Courtly World of Bourbon Spain," unpublished paper presented at the Boston University Domenico Scarlatti Festival, February 19–21, 1998. See also Nigel Glendinning, *A Literary History of Spain: The Eighteenth Century* (London: Ernest Benn Limited, 1972); and John Lynch, *Bourbon Spain (1700–1808)* (Oxford: Basil Blackwell, 1989).

[58] For a thorough study of Crotch and his aesthetics, see Howard Irving, *Ancients and Moderns: William Crotch and the Development of Classical Music* (Aldershot: Ashgate, 1999).

the object of imitation in other composers."[59] He says the same thing, a bit more harshly, twenty years later, in 1831, writing: "Some great men, as Domenico Scarlatti, have occasionally endeavoured to dispense with the rules; but it may be questioned whether anything great, or worthy of imitation, was ever the result."[60] Nevertheless, Crotch does include a sonata by Scarlatti in his *Specimens on Various Styles of Music*, the *Sonata in D Major*, K. 2, first published in the *Essercizi*, a copy of which Crotch probably owned.[61]

This discomfort with composers who "transgressed the rules" or dispensed with them entirely was shared by many of the leading British musicians and writers of this time, and even extended to Haydn, a man and composer they greatly admired, because of the unusual shifts in melody, harmony, and form often found in his works. Charles Burney would thus write in 1791: "We are not certain that our present musical doctors and graduates are *quite up* to Haydn yet."[62] He expanded on this criticism in a letter to Crotch of February 17, 1805, complaining about Haydn's "whimsicalities, which he sometimes introduced for the sake of variety." Referring to Haydn's "wit," "sport," and playfulness, Burney questions whether "enough [would] remain of serious, beautiful & sublime, to constitute a great man."[63] The same question and adjectives he used to describe Haydn could have just as easily been applied to Scarlatti and his music.

In point of fact, both Haydn and Scarlatti were viewed as a bit too "picturesque," as defined by Uvedale Price in his 1794 *An Essay on the Picturesque*, in which he draws a parallel between what he called the picturesque in painting (i.e., "quaint scenes such as ruins, gnarled oaks, cart-horses and peasants . . . sudden, unexpected, and abrupt transitions [and] a certain playful wildness of character, and an appearance of irregularity") with music.[64] It is not surprising that Crotch uses this term to criticize Scarlatti, calling him "the father of that style which we have denominated

---

[59] William Crotch, *Elements of Musical Composition* (London: Longman, Hurst, Rees, Orme, & Brown, 1812), p. 28, cited in Bernarr Rainbow, *Four Centuries of Teaching Manuals, 1518–1932* (Woodbridge: The Boydell Press, 1992), p. 110.

[60] William Crotch, *Substance of Several Courses of Lectures on Music, Read in the University of Oxford and in the Metropolis* (London: Longman, Rees, Orme, Brown, and Green, 1831), p. 12.

[61] William Crotch, *Specimens on Various Styles of Music Referred to in a Course of Lectures, Read at Oxford and London, and Adapted to Keyed Instruments* (London: R. Birchall, ca. 1815). It appears as example no. 9 on pages 6–9.

[62] Cited in Simon McVeigh, *Concert Life in London from Mozart to Haydn* (Cambridge: Cambridge University Press, 1993), p. 160, quoting Landon, *Haydn in England*, p. 103.

[63] Cited in McVeigh, *Concert Life in London from Mozart to Haydn*, pp. 160–161, as found in Burney, *A General History*, vol. ii, pp. 1033–1034.

[64] Uvedale Price, *An Essay on the Picturesque, as Compared with the Sublime and the Beautiful*, rev. ed. (London, 1796–8), vol. 1, pp. 55–56, cited in McVeigh, *Concert Life in London from Mozart to Haydn*, p. 160. It is also no coincidence that the "Picturesque" is closely linked to the Gothic revivals in architecture and literature. For a discussion of the picturesque in music, particularly as applied to the fantasias of C. P. E. Bach, see Annette Richards, *The Free Fantasia and the Musical Picturesque* (Cambridge: Cambridge University Press, 2001).

the ornamental or picturesque."[65] Price points to *both* Haydn and Scarlatti as "picturesque" composers, leading to the conclusion that Burney might have been right: British "musical doctors and graduates" were not ready for either "rule breaker."

It would therefore be almost a century after the British publication of Scarlatti's *Essercizi* and the initial forays into Scarlatti's music by the "sect" before his sonatas began to return to the repertoire. This was due in great part to Moscheles, as mentioned previously, who began by performing (as listed in the program) "Suites of Lessons (including the celebrated 'Cat's Fugue')" by Scarlatti at the first concert of his "historical soirées" on February 18, 1837.[66] What made his performances even more notable is that Moscheles played the sonatas not only on a harpsichord, the program proudly specifying "as originally written for the Harpsichord and, by desire, performed on that instrument by Mr. Moscheles," but on a so-called period instrument, a two-manual Schudi-Broadwood harpsichord that, according to Moscheles' wife Charlotte, was "built in the year 1771, and still in possession of Messrs. Broadwood." Moscheles, moreover, mentions a special feature of this instrument, a Venetian Swell stop, that he praised for the "greater sonority ... given to the tone," although he did call the sound of all harpsichords "rather thin, and less agreeable," a comment one might expect from a pianist familiar with Erards, Grafs, and similar grand pianos.[67]

In their comments about the event, Moscheles (and/or Charlotte) made another error of judgment about the harpsichord regarding the two keyboards of the Broadwood harpsichord, assuming that "the upper and lower keyboards of the instrument were evidently intended for the rendering of such passages of Scarlatti and other masters as on modern pianos require constant crossing of the hands."[68] This is, of course, an understandable mistake, considering the rarity of the use of the harpsichord, or even its appearance on the concert stage during the late 1830s, at least as a solo instrument.[69] The error was publicly corrected many

---

[65] Irving, *Ancients and Moderns*, p. 148.   [66] See Kroll, *Ignaz Moscheles*, pp. 286–287.

[67] See Ignatz [sic] Moscheles, *Recent Music and Musicians, Edited by His Wife and Adapted from the Original German by A. D. Coleridge* (New York: Henry Holt and Company, 1873), to be further cited as *RMM*, p. 236. Most critics of the time had a low opinion of the instrument, such as Henry Robertson, who complained in 1809 that "the clicking of the quills, and the whistling of the cords, render the recitative more than usually unpleasant," and *The Morning Chronicle* in 1817, which criticized "the miserable fiction of a jingling harpsichord." See Holman, *Life after Death*, pp. 311–312.

[68] Moscheles, *RMM*, pp. 236–237.

[69] The harpsichord was certainly used in public prior to Moscheles' performance in 1837, but only as a continuo instrument and not in a solo capacity. For example, Peter Holman tells us that "Vincenzo Pucitta was advertised as 'Composer and Conductor (at the harpsichord) of the Music' in two comic operas put on at the King's Theatre" in 1809, Vincent Novello played a harpsichord in 1812, and the instrument appeared in London auctions in 1820 and 1828. See Holman, *Life after Death*, pp. 311–312.

years later by Moscheles' former student A. J. Hipkins in a series of lectures given between 1885 and 1886. Hipkins starts out with a small mistake of his own: "Scarlatti wrote, I believe, for the single keyboard harpsichord." We now know that Scarlatti had a wide range of keyboard instruments available to him in the Lisbon and Madrid courts, including two-manual harpsichords, clavi-chords, and pianos.[70] However, Hipkins was correct in observing that Scarlatti "crossed his hands exactly as we now cross them in playing the pianoforte," calling it one of the Scarlatti trademarks, and went on by gently disabusing his teacher's notion that "this crossing of the hands in Scarlatti's harpsichord pieces did really signify, in some unexplained way, the use of two keyboards."[71]

Moscheles would perform a good number of Scarlatti sonatas throughout his career, on both harpsichord and piano. In addition to the "Cats' Fugue" (i.e., the *Sonata in G Minor*, K. 30), they include the following (as listed in his programs): "Fugue in D minor published in CLEMENTI'S *Practical Harmony*" (i.e., the *Sonata in D Minor*, K. 41); "Suites of Lessons" by Scarlatti; and "Lento pasticio et allegro, from the lessons of Scarlatti" (unidentifiable). Moscheles also evoked Scarlatti in the etude no. 10 of his first book of piano etudes, op. 70, writing that it was composed "in the ancient Style (somewhat in that of Scarlatti)" and was intended for the uniform execution of trills with "a rapid and elastic change [of] fingers" without "disturbing in the least the quiet and stately character of the whole."[72] Moscheles and Fétis also included a work by Scarlatti in their *Méthode des Méthodes*, the *Sonata in F Major*, K. 366, listed as an *Etude Composée Par Domenico Scarlatti*.[73]

---

[70] See Kirkpatrick, *Domenico Scarlatti*, pp. 175–185 and 361–363.

[71] A. J. Hipkins, "The Old Clavier or Keyboard Instruments; Their Use by Composers, and Technique." *Proceedings of the Musical Association, 12th Sess. (1885–1886)*, pp. 139–148, here p. 144.

[72] Ignaz Moscheles, *Studien für das Pianoforte*, op. 70 (Leipzig: Friedrich Kistner, n.d.), p. 47, English version taken from Carew, *The Mechanical Muse*, pp. 180–181, citing the Augener edition of 1870. The "Ancient Style" was often used by composers of this era to describe pieces that were intended to evoke early music. Other examples include J. B. Cramer's *The Two Styles: Ancient and Modern* (1842), a piano piece with "Stile Antico and Stile Moderno, hearkening back to French overtures and other stylistic elements (see Carew, *The Mechanical Muse*, p. 176); in Cipriano Potter's fourth study in B-flat minor of his first book of piano studies (1826), which he directs to be played in *stile antico* (see Carew, *The Mechanical Muse*, p. 179); and Moscheles own "A gigue, or dance movement, in the old style, for the piano-forte, composed purposely for The Harmonicon," published in *The Harmonicon*, 1823, vol. I, no. 33, part II, and Gb-Lbl, P.P. 1947. See Kroll, *Ignaz Moscheles*, p. 349.

[73] F. J. Fétis and J. Moscheles, *Méthode des Méthodes* (Paris: Maurice Schlesinger, 1840; facs. ed. Minkoff Reprint, Genève, 1973), p. 104.

Scarlatti after 1850[74]

Scarlatti's sonatas did occasionally appear on piano recitals after 1850, but almost always as an opening piece for a much larger selection of "real" piano music that would follow. For example, Clara Schumann's recital at the Queen's Concert Rooms, Hanover Square, on June 17, 1856, included a "Clavierstück in A major" by Scarlatti. The remaining pieces on the program were by Beethoven, Brahms, Robert Schumann, W. S. Bennett, and Clara herself.[75]

Nevertheless, some pianists after 1850 did not treat early music, including Scarlatti's sonatas, as a throwaway or afterthought. One was the Moscheles student and Austrian émigré to England Ernst Pauer (1826–1905), who played sonatas by Domenico Scarlatti in 1861 in his series "Historical Performances of Pianoforte Music in strictly Chronological Order," and more Scarlatti among his historical recitals in 1863 and 1867 that also included music by Porpora, Mattheson, Handel, J. S. Bach and sons, F. Couperin, and Rameau.[76] According to Alfred Hipkins, Pauer also played on the same 1771 Schudi harpsichord used by Moscheles in 1837 in his own concerts of 1863 and 1867.[77]

William Sterndale Bennett (1816–1875) played works by Scarlatti on March 13, 1853, as part of his "Annual Series of Classical Pianoforte Concerts," and Charles Salaman (1814–1901) began a series of harpsichord concerts in 1855 that included music of Scarlatti, often playing them on his own 1768 Kirkman instrument.[78] For a program in 1862, however, Salaman used the Schudi harpsichord that Moscheles had played, the *Musical World* writing: "Mr. Salaman gave marked interest to his concert by performing solos from Handel and Scarlatti upon a double harpsichord, manufactured by Tschudi, the predecessor of Broadwood; upon just such an instrument, in fact, as both those composers must have themselves used."[79] Several decades later, in 1886,

---

[74] Since a musical era does not neatly confine itself to dates on a calendar, each section of this Element will conclude with a discussion of the events relevant to Bach, Handel, and Scarlatti that occurred in the years following our admittedly artificial cutoff of 1850.

[75] Janet Ritterman and William Weber, "Origins of the Piano Recital in England, 1830–1870," in *The Piano in Nineteenth-Century British Culture: Instruments, Performers and Repertoire*, eds. Therese Ellsworth and Susan Wollenberg (Aldershot: Ashgate, 2007), p. 182, the source being Clara Wieck Schumann, *Sammlung der Konzertprogramme*, Robert Schumann Haus, Zwickau, Sign. 10463-A3.

[76] See Harry Haskell, *The Early Music Revival*, p. 21; Dorothy de Val and Cyril Ehrlich, "Repertory and Canon," in *The Cambridge Companion to the Piano*, ed. David Rowland (Cambridge: Cambridge University Press, 1998), p. 129; Kroll, *Ignaz Moscheles*, p. 304; *The Musical World*, March 6, 1861 (39:11), p. 171; and *The Musical World*, April 25, 1863, p. 266.

[77] See Holman, *Life after Death*, p. 320, citing Hipkins, *Grove 1*, ii p. 96; and Edward Kottick, *A History of the Harpsichord* (Bloomington: Indiana University Press, 2003), pp. 398–399.

[78] For Bennett, see Kroll, *Ignaz Moscheles*, p. 303, and *The Musical World*, March 17, 1853 (33:11), p. 172. For Salaman, see Kroll, *Ignaz Moscheles*, p. 304.

[79] *The Musical World*, June 21, 1862 (40:25), p. 389. See Kroll, *Ignaz Moscheles*, p. 304, fn. 132.

Florence May performed Scarlatti (on piano), as well as "works by Couperin, Rameau . . . Alberti, Symonds, Greene, Handel, [and] Bach," plus the standard repertoire of the time: music of Beethoven, Mendelssohn, Weber, Schumann, Chopin, Brahms, Liszt, and Moscheles.[80]

Ironically, a major boost on behalf of Scarlatti would have to wait until the last half of the nineteenth century, from none other than Johannes Brahms, himself a passionate antiquarian who reportedly owned 308 Scarlatti sonatas from the collection of the Abbé Santini.[81] Brahms even used the opening measures of the *Sonata in D Major*, K. 223 (see Ex. 10) to begin his song *Unüberwindlich*, op. 72, no. 5 (see Ex. 11).

It was not until the twentieth century, however, that, thanks to the scholarship and editorial work of Ralph Kirkpatrick, Emilia Fadini, Malcolm Boyd, Kenneth Gilbert, and others, these masterpieces of the harpsichord literature would once again be recognized as an important element of the early-music canon.[82]

3 George Frederic Handel

The Handel Commemoration of 1834 was as impressive a spectacle as were its predecessors some fifty years earlier. It was, in fact, so memorable that Ignaz Moscheles devoted four pages to the event in his diaries, describing a sumptuous affair that included a total of 625 musicians – 223 instrumentalists, a chorus of 397 singers, and five soloists – performing for an audience of 2,700 in "seats covered with red cloth and gold ornaments [that] contrasted tastefully with the white and gold lyres on red draperies, which were hung upon the walls." Moscheles added that the impact of the event was so great that "the newspapers talked of several ladies weeping, and some actually fainting," and confessed that he personally was "deeply moved by these sounds," having "never heard such an effect produced before."[83]

---

[80] Kroll, *Ignaz Moscheles*, p. 305, and *The Musical World*, October 30, 1886, p. 701.

[81] See Kirkpatrick, *Domenico Scarlatti*, p. 139. The collection is now housed in the *Gesellschaft der Musikfreunde* in Vienna.

[82] William Weber describes three categories of canon in musical culture: "scholarly," "pedagogical," and "performing." We encounter the creation of all three in Britain between 1750 and 1850. See William Weber, "The History of Musical Canon," in *Rethinking Music*, eds. Nicholas Cook and Mark Everist (Oxford: Oxford University Press, 1999), pp. 336–355, here pp. 339–340.

[83] See Moscheles, *RMM*, pp. 202–206 and Kroll, *Ignaz Moscheles*, pp. 275–276. The conductor of the event, Sir George Smart, recorded his own figures for all four concerts of the 1834 Commemoration, and they are indeed impressive:

"Total Performers:	1st 602	2nd 603	3rd 611	4th 599
Band:	222	222	224	222
Chorus:	316	316	316	316
Semi-chorus:	40	40	40	40
Organists:	2	2	2	1

Orchestra: 80 violins, 32 viola, 18 cellos, 18 double basses, 10 flutes, 12 oboes, 8 clarinets, 12 bassoons, 10 horns, 8 trumpet, 8 trombones, 2 ophicleide, 2 serpents, 2 side

Example 10 Domenico Scarlatti, *Sonata in D Major*, K. 223, mm. 1–4

Example 11 Johannes Brahms, *Unüberwindlich*, op. 72, no. 5, mm. 1–4

It is not surprising that Moscheles, the German-speaking immigrant from Bohemia and Austria who came to love and admire almost every aspect of his adopted country, was overwhelmed by the effects he had never before heard. The British seem to have a special knack at putting on and presenting royal pageants on the grandest of scales, and the Handel commemorations belong to that category. One can only imagine what the massive performing forces actually sounded like in the generous acoustics of Westminster Abbey in 1834. It must have indeed been overwhelming, as it was in the previous Handel commemorations of the eighteenth century.[84] Fortunately, we might be able to get a sense of what Moscheles and his fellow audience members experienced by comparing it with a modern celebration that was seen and heard around the world: the coronation of Queen Elizabeth II on June 2, 1953, which was watched on television by 27 million people in the United Kingdom (out of a total population of 36 million), listened to on the radio by another 11 million, and broadcast internationally throughout the Commonwealth.

The 1834 festival, essentially a commemoration of a commemoration, was indeed one of those magnificent musical displays and more, as was the original

---

drums, 1 timpani, 1 tower timpani." Cited in John Carnelly, *George Smart and 19th-Century London Concert Life* (Woodbridge: The Boydell Press, 2015), p. 199.

[84] The concept of "bigger is better" when it came to Handel did not apply merely to volume level, but rather to the view of Handel as being "sublime." See Claudia L. Johnson, "'Giant HANDEL' and the Musical Sublime," *Eighteenth-Century Studies*, vol. 19, no. 4 (Summer, 1996), pp. 515–533. Johnson writes that Burney was "proud of the gigantic proportions Handel's music assumed," and cautions today's historical performers who "try to reconstruct smaller and supposedly more historically 'correct' productions" that "eighteenth-century listeners, far from considering smallness a standard of correctness, show a discomforting fondness for overpowering dimensions."

1784 Festival and the five Handel commemorations that followed in rapid succession (1785, 1786, 1787, 1790, and 1791).[85] These, as we discussed in the Introduction, were intentional and ostentatious expressions of political and economic power, a "conspicuous example of propagandist royal pageantry" that explains why, as Simon McVeigh observes, it was the king who "wanted to maintain the festival when the directors sought to discontinue it in 1792."[86] The festivals went even further, according to McVeigh and William Weber, becoming "a national ritual," a forum for a "confirmation of establishment values, based around a conservative political consensus, the Anglican church and ... British patriotism [plus an] established social order hallowed by tradition."[87]

It is also not surprising that as British power and wealth grew, so did the festivals. By the time of the festival of 1791, which was attended by Haydn, there were 1,067 participants.[88] Counting the audience, the actual number of people crowded into Westminster Abbey on May 26, 1791, was more than twice that, Marsh estimating "about 2200 people." However, he had some reservations about this large number of performers, particularly about the balance between the "band," which had been augmented "to a very great degree," with a large chorus that had admitted "chorus singers from most of the country choirs in England." This, Marsh felt, "had crowded & encumber'd the orchestra without improving the effect," which he compared unfavorably to "the original Commemoration of Handel in 1784, when the band consisted of about 500 vocal and instrumental performers."[89] Marsh's objections to such large and unbalanced performing forces would usually not be voiced in the early nineteenth century, when the number of people on the stage seemed to expand without limit.

---

[85] These events could also sometimes be a delight not only for the ears, but also for the eyes, especially for those of the more lecherous male members of the audience. In his report from the 1784 Commemoration, John Marsh tells us that when the maids of honor, wearing their "great hoops," had to climb "over the back seats to come at those in front of the box provided for them ... they display'd their *understandings* [italics original] to the admiring prebendaries just under them." Marsh also noted with amusement that one of these prebendaries even put on his glasses ("spectacled") to get a better view. *The John Marsh Journals*, p. 317.

[86] Simon McVeigh, *Concert Life in London from Mozart to Haydn* (Cambridge: Cambridge University Press, 1993), p. 25.

[87] McVeigh, *Concert Life in London*, p. 25. The 1834 Commemoration was no less political, coming on the heels of the 1832 reform bill. Formally titled *An Act to Amend the Representation of the People in England and Wales*, it made major changes to the electoral system in England and Wales.

[88] McVeigh, *Concert Life in London*, p. 24. Two other attendees were teenage boys who would later achieve lasting fame and recognition: Johann Nepomuk Hummel and George Bridgetower. In 1791 they stood on either side of the organist, Joah Bates, to help him change the registrations. Hummel would go on to enjoy a major career as a pianist and composer. Bridgetower would later play the premiere and become the dedicatee of Beethoven's *Sonata for Violin and Piano*, op. 47 ("Kreutzer"). See Kroll, *Johann Nepomuk Hummel*, p. 35.

[89] *The John Marsh Journals*, pp. 493–494.

Nonmusical activities could also sometimes drown out the music of Handel, at least symbolically, especially considering the complex political and social forces at play, and their often-conflicting ideologies. One, of a religious nature, did just that on June 23, 1791, during a performance of *Messiah*, when, as Marsh recalls: "Just as Sign'a Storace was making her concluding cadence to the air 'I know that my Redeemer liveth' a young female Quaker sitting under the Dean called out 'Fie upon it, it's high idolatory.'" Marsh was clearly not unfamiliar with the various religious controversies bubbling on top or simmering within British society. On this occasion, he did not seem to be greatly bothered by the Quaker's demonstration, calmly and cynically observing that, satisfied by the "bustle [she] created" with her outburst, "she coolly went out of the church with a friend she had treated with a ticket," the two having attended for the sole purpose of speaking their mind.[90] One can safely assume that the performance went on undisturbed. Similar religious conflicts emerged during the 1834 Commemoration, one result being that none of the Dissenting Choirs in London were invited to participate.[91]

Other nonmusical events, however, were not ideological or religious, but nevertheless potentially life-threatening, even if they were the result of something as innocent as the improper construction of a structure to accommodate the large number of performers. One such instance that occurred during a performance of *Messiah* at the Drury Lane Theater in 1786 tells us something about the skill, or the lack thereof, of English carpenters. Between the second and third acts of the oratorio, as related by Parke, "the upper tier, on which were stationed the trumpets, French-horns, bassoons, and kettle-drums, suddenly gave way, and the performers who were on it were precipitated down a descent of fourteen feet." Apparently there were no serious injuries, perhaps because, as the old cliché goes, there *was* a doctor in the house, Parke explaining: "Nelson, the pompous kettle-drummer, who had escaped unhurt, strutting about with his usual dignity, said to those who lay sprawling on the floor, 'Gentlemen! if any of you have broken a limb, make yourselves perfectly easy, for Mr. Pott, the celebrated surgeon, is in the pit.'"[92]

It was inevitable, of course, that there would be some musical friction at these massive and highly public concerts, particularly given the number of egos

---

[90] *The John Marsh Journals*, p. 521.

[91] See Weber, *The Rise of Musical Classics in Eighteenth-Century England*, p. 141. For further information on these choirs and religious dissent in general, see Nicholas Temperley, "The Music of Dissent," in Isabel Rivers and David L. Wykes, *Dissenting Praise: Religious Dissent and the Hymn in England and Wales* (Oxford: Oxford University Press, 2011), chapter 8.

[92] Parke, *Musical Memoirs*, p. 65.

involved. One concerned the question of who was to lead the "band" (i.e., serve as the conductor), a role usually assumed by the first violinist for choral music at this time. This problem, which did not seem to get fully resolved for any genre or repertoire until the middle of the nineteenth century, was certainly present at the 1784 Commemoration, at least according to William Parke. He writes about two distinguished guests, the Oxford music professor Dr. Philip Hayes (1738–1797) and the Doncaster organist Dr. Edward Miller (1731 or 1735–1807), appearing unannounced and apparently uninvited to conduct the first perform-ance. Parke vividly describes the reaction of the first violinist, Wilhelm Cramer (1746–1799), who, after tapping his bow to give the signal for the orchestra to start, "saw, to his astonishment, a tall gigantic figure, with an immense pow-dered toupee, full dressed, with a bag and sword, and a huge roll of parchment in his hand." Cramer asked: "Who is that gentleman?" and when informed it was the illustrious professor Hayes who had come "to beat time," he unceremoni-ously announced that he would begin only when he "has sat down." Apparently, Dr. Professor Hayes meekly did as instructed.[93]

Unfortunately, as colorful and irresistible as this anecdote might be, it appears to be incorrect, at least in terms of the 1784 Handel Commemoration. According to Peter Holman, it was not mentioned by Burney or in any of the other eyewitness accounts, leading to the conclusion that Parke might have confused it with a similar event at the first New Musical Fund concert at the Haymarket Theatre on April 12, 1787, or in St. Paul's during a Festival of the Sons of the Clergy, with Charles Ashley as leader rather than Cramer.[94] Wherever it took place, or if at all, Parke's comments underscore the pervasive and problematic issue of who was to lead a large ensemble or chorus, one that remained a source of discussion and change until the 1840s.

Nevertheless, despite previous problems with conductors, carpenters, lecher-ous prebendaries, religious dissenters, Quakers, and a host of other issues, the grandeur of the 1834 Commemoration, and the fact that it was held at all almost eighty years after the composer's death, confirms that Handel remained the same iconic musical figure in Britain in the first half of the nineteenth century that he was in the eighteenth, at least to a certain degree. However, although icons rarely if ever lose their stature, their image is often subject to revision and reinterpretation, and this is certainly true when we examine the reception of

---

[93] Parke, *Musical Memoirs*, pp. 39–40.

[94] See Peter Holman, *Before the Baton: Musical Direction and Conducting in Stuart and Georgian Britain* (Woodbridge: The Boydell Press, 2020), pp. 162 and 165; Parke, *Musical Memoirs*, I, p. 98; and Peter Holman, "The Conductor at the Organ, or How Choral and Orchestral Music Was Directed in Georgian England," in *Music and Performance Culture in Nineteenth-Century Britain: Essays in Honour of Nicholas Temperley*, ed. Bennett Zon (Farnham: Ashgate, 2012), pp. 243–261, here pp. 255–256.

Handel's music after his death: it never lost its luster, but changed over succeeding generations, and especially during the period from 1750 to 1850.

One aspect of that change might seem surprising and even self-contradictory, considering the extraordinary events celebrating Handel's music: interest in his large oratorios was quickly fading, even before 1784. Simply put, many concertgoers found them dull and out of date. For example, in 1775 Mrs. James Harris wrote to her son: "your father and I went yesterday to the oratorio in the Haymarket; your sisters are too refined for 'old Handel.'"[95] In 1782 the author of an article in the *Westminster Magazine* bemoaned the fact that "once a year ... a few of the Oratorios are performed; but all their thunder, majesty, and strength, is scarcely sufficient to keep the audience awake, which, to say the truth, is for the most part so thin, that it cannot be for the interest of a manager to continue these entertainments any longer."[96]

It would be surprising to hear similar comments from Charles Burney, an English musical chauvinist to the end, and a lifelong Handel booster. Writing about the "second class of English masters of the sixteenth century," he quoted "a worthy Nobleman" who declared that "there is doubtless more nerve, more science, and fire, in the worst of Handel's choruses, than in the greatest efforts of these old madrigalists."[97] Nevertheless, Burney himself seems to have seen this trend developing, even during the opening days of the 1784 Commemoration, writing to Sir Joseph Banks on May 26, 1784, that the public was "heartily tired of [Handel oratorios]" because they had heard them too often. He repeated his reservations in 1791, assuming that neither the wealthy nor the enthusiasts would want to attend "such an expensive performance year after year, merely to hear the same pieces repeated."[98] John Marsh also noted this phenomenon in his diaries, lamenting from the vantage point of 1807 about "the languor, with which the oratorios of Handel were carried on in Lent a little more than twenty years ago."[99]

This precipitous posthumous change in Handel's musical fortunes can be traced to a number of factors, all of which reflect the transformation from the baroque to classical styles that was happening during this time, as well as changes in audience behavior and attitudes. They include a growing preference for simpler

---

[95] William Weber, *The Rise of Musical Classics*, p. 124, citing an entry of March 10, 1775, in *Diaries and Correspondence of James Harris, First Earl of Malmesbury*, 4 vols. (London, 1844), vol. I, p. 293.

[96] Weber, *The Rise of Musical Classics*, p. 124.

[97] Charles Burney, *A General History of Music*, vol. ii, p. 112. Burney's comparisons of Handel with J. S. Bach were even more negative, as we will read in the next section.

[98] McVeigh, *Concert Life in London*, p. 98, quoting Christopher Hogwood, *Handel* (London: Thames & Hudson, 1988), p. 245.

[99] Cited in McVeigh, *Concert Life in London*, p. 31.

(e.g., two-voice) textures, the rise of independent instrumental music, an increasing secularization with the advent of a growing middle class, and of course, the increasing dominance of Mozart and Haydn on concert programs.

A number of Handel's grand oratorios still attracted audiences, of course, and perhaps also kept them awake.[100] *Messiah* never lost its appeal, and its loyal advocates remained steadfast, such as Moscheles, who would write excitedly about an upcoming performance of the work in his diary as late as 1833: "I swallowed my dinner hastily, so as not to miss a note of this masterpiece."[101] *Israel in Egypt* was another mainstay in the Handel repertoire, although it too suffered from declining interest: despite being featured in the concert of May 23 at the final Handel Commemoration of 1791, it had received only a single additional performance that year, on April 13.[102] The *Dettingen Te Deum* is yet another large-scale Handel choral work that seemed to retain its place on programs.

A few of the lighter secular works also survived, such as *Alexander's Feast*, *L'Allegro, Il Penseroso, ed Il Moderato*, and *Acis and Galatea* in particular, although it too was subject to the vagaries of taste. When it was performed at Drury Lane on March 24, 1784, according to *The Public Advertiser*, "the House, to the Disgrace of our idle People, was very indifferent indeed."[103] Nevertheless, this remarkable, sturdy, and relatively short dramatic work (by Handelian standards) took on a healthy life of its own, attracting a loyal audience. Moscheles was one of them, as demonstrated in a diary entry for June 22, 1829: "One of the choicest entertainments this season was the dramatized representation of Handel's 'Acis and Galatea,' performed at Bochsa's concert; the music allotted to the chief characters was admirably sung by Miss Paton and Braham; Zuccheli, with a gigantic eye in the middle of his forehead, was a very good Polyphemus."[104] *Acis and Galatea* would remain one of the most popular of Handel's works in England for decades, being presented as revivals in "concert form," and in burlesque or parody versions.[105]

---

[100] According to McVeigh, another sign of the changing times with regards to Handel's oratorios was the frequent insertion of concertos and other "virtuoso showpieces performed by imported soloists between the acts." Clearly entertainment value supplanted Handel idolatry. McVeigh, *Concert Life in London*, p. 31.

[101] *RMM*, p. 196 and Kroll, *Ignaz Moscheles*, p. 274. Nevertheless, Moscheles still had to endure some unsatisfying performances of this and other Handel oratorios during this period. After listening to a performance of Handel's *Solomon* in 1839, he told his diary that he would simply not let "that glorious work ... be spoiled by the organ being below pitch, painful as it was." Moscheles, *RMM*, p. 262 and Kroll, *Ignaz Moscheles*, p. 276.

[102] McVeigh, *Concert Life in London*, p. 32.

[103] McVeigh, *Concert Life in London*, p. 31, citing *The Public Advertiser*, March 26, 1784.

[104] Moscheles, *RMM*, p. 153 and Kroll, *Ignaz Moscheles*, p. 274.

[105] Such versions were presented at the Adelphi Theater (Strand, London) on February 8, 1842; the Olympic Theater (Strand, London) on March 7, 1842; and the Royal Olympic Theater (Strand, London) on April 6, 1863. See Roberta Montemorra Marvin, "Handel's *Acis and Galatea*:

What did change, but what also kept the major Handel oratorio repertoire from disappearing completely, was the increasing use of excerpts rather than full performances. For example, by 1785 the pension fund for the city's musicians at the Royal Theatre began putting on concerts of arias from different works by Handel, but not complete oratorios. Tellingly, a concert at the King's Theater on February 24, 1791, featured such excerpts as the "CHORUS, 'Gird on thy Sword,'" "He gave them Hailstones," and "RECITATIVE AND CHORUS 'Sing ye to the Lord,'" plus a (presumably complete) performance of Haydn's 'GRAND SYMPHONY.'"[106] By 1825, the program for the "First Concert" of the "Antient Concert" on March 2 conducted by Sir George Smart consisted of thirteen pieces by Handel, but all were excerpts. (The concert also included an oboe concerto and a "Movement from his Lessons.")[107] The festivals of The Sons of the Clergy were also usually dominated by Handelian excerpts, such as the overture to *Esther*, the "Hallelujah Chorus," and *Zadok the Priest*.[108] This did not please many members of the British musical community, including Moscheles, who objected to "the English practice of performing only selections from Handel's oratorios, rather than the complete work." He considered that "to a German musician [this] was an offence," and following his instincts about always respecting the composer's intentions, or at least trying to, advocated for complete performances of Handel's works: "The effect of such performances would be enhanced, if the oratorios were given, not piecemeal, but in their entirety, just as the composer intended they should be given."[109]

However, despite his protestations about honoring the composer's intentions, Moscheles, like almost every other musician of this era, never hesitated in making changes to the originals, in terms of musical text, size of ensemble, and orchestration. This included using an ophicleide in his beloved *Messiah*, as he described in a letter to Mendelssohn on June 26, 1834, after hearing it used in a performance of the oratorio that year, writing that it was "a very useful addition, for just as you say of a steam engine, it has ten-horse power, so of this you can say, it has ten-trombone power."[110]

A Victorian View," in *Europe, Empire, and Spectacle in Nineteenth-Century British Music*, eds. Rachel Cowgill and Julian Rushton (Aldershot: Ashgate, 2006), pp. 249–264.

[106] See facsimile of the program in McVeigh, *Concert Life in London*, p. 74.

[107] Carnelly, *George Smart and 19th-Century London Concert Life*, p. 75.

[108] McVeigh, *Concert Life in London*, p. 97.

[109] Moscheles, *RMM*, p. 206 and Kroll, *Ignaz Moscheles*, p. 276. Moscheles' insistence that German musicians did not program excerpts is an exaggeration. A similar practice can be found in many German and other continental countries, as we noted in the Introduction with our description of the "historical concert" presented by *Euterpe* in Leipzig in 1835.

[110] *Letters of Felix Mendelssohn to Ignaz and Charlotte Moscheles: Translated from the Originals in His Possession, and Edited by Felix Moscheles* (Freeport, NY: Books for Libraries Press, 1970), p. 117.

Not surprisingly, excerpts of Handel also dominated the programming of the Royal Philharmonic, that is, when it did include a work by the composer, which was not very often, since like most orchestras even today, it never devoted much if any attention to early music. As an examination of the list of programs from 1818 to 1895 reveals, the Philharmonic did not present a single performance of a complete oratorio or any Handel vocal work during a period of almost eighty years – all were excerpts (see Appendix 1 for a complete list). However, Handel oratorios in their original and complete versions did seem to enjoy a healthy afterlife in some of the major provincial cities of Britain. For example, the Liverpool Festival of 1787 featured a complete *Israel in Egypt*, and William Crotch conducted more than 200 performers in Mozart's arrangement of *Messiah* in October 1808 at the Birmingham Festival.[111] Handel's *Dettingen Te Deum* was the featured work at the Norwich Festival on September 22, 1824 (although only excerpts), and the Birmingham Festival presented a complete *Messiah* on October 10, 1832, and a full performance of *Israel in Egypt* on October 11, using 300 performers accompanied by Birmingham's new four-manual organ.[112]

As mentioned in the Introduction, academic institutions, notably Oxford University, played an important role in keeping Handel and his music on a pedestal – as they do to this day.[113] For example, according to Susan Wollenberg, a convocation held to honor the benefactors of the university in 1754 "took on the appearance of a Handel festival," with performances of *L'Allegro, Il Penseroso ed Il Moderato, Judas Maccabaeus,* and *Messiah* at the Sheldonian Theatre on July 3–5 of that year.[114] Another three day mini festival at Oxford took place between June 5 and 7, 1788, featuring "*Acis and Galatea* at the Sheldonian on the Wednesday, *Messiah* for the anniversary of the Radcliffe Infirmary on the Thursday, and a 'Grand Miscellaneous Concert' at the Sheldonian on the Friday."[115] *Acis and Galatea* was again performed at Oxford, on February 18, 1805, the performers' names being handwritten on the program.[116] Not surprisingly, by 1819, excerpts dominated the Handel concert

---

[111] Pippa Drummond, *The Provincial Music Festival in England, 1784–1914* (Surrey: Ashgate, 2011), pp. 29 and 26 respectively.

[112] Drummond, *The Provincial Music Festival in England, 1784–1914*, pp. 43 and 68 respectively.

[113] That is, many of the early-music/historical performance advocates today began their explorations into this repertoire, including Scarlatti and Bach, in the 1960s and 1970s while students at various universities in Great Britain and the United States.

[114] Susan Wollenberg. "Music in 18th-Century Oxford," in *Proceedings of the Royal Musical Association*, vol. 108 (1981–1982), pp. 69–99, here p. 73 and p. 80 n. 32, citing Oxford, Bodleian Library, MS Top. Oxon. d. 247, p. 114, July 2, 1754.

[115] Wollenberg, *Music in 18th-Century Oxford*, p. 81.

[116] See a facsimile of that program in Susan Wollenberg, *Music at Oxford in the Eighteenth and Nineteenth Centuries* (Oxford: Oxford University Press, 2001), p. 148.

at the Oxford Music Room on June 22 of that year, with the program listing "Overture, Samson," "Chorus 'Awake the trumpet's lofty sound,'" "Song – Miss Stephens 'Thou didst blow,'" "Chorus, 'The depths have covered them,'" "Chorus, 'O Father, whose almighty power,'" and "Chorus 'When his loud voice.'"[117]

Another development during this era was a growing emphasis on Handel's operas. Not the full multi-hour version, of course, but only selections and individual arias, in keeping with the trends in oratorio performances and concertgoing in general. The Concert of Antient Music, for example, brought back far more of Handel's opera arias than were encountered anywhere else; fully a third of the pieces by Handel performed during the period were excerpts from his operas.[118] This brand of musical "downsizing" can also be seen in the proliferation of arrangements that began to flood the market, even more than were published during Handel's lifetime, presumably in response to the demand from a growing and enthusiastic middle class that wanted to play this music in the privacy of their own homes.[119] Although this also helped to keep the music of Handel and other composers relevant in the contemporary musical scene, the technique often drew some scathing criticism. A good example is this sarcastic description of multiple arrangements of the opera *Semiramide* by a later but equally famous composer of opera, Rossini, which appeared in *The Athenaeum* in 1828: "No sooner is an opera out, but to instant work fall the legions of arrangers and adapters. Out comes *Semiramide*, arranged for the pianoforte; *Semiramide* arranged for the pianoforte and flute; *Semiramide* arranged for a single tiny flute; and for aught we know, *Semiramide* arranged for the French horn or the Jew's-harp." The writer concluded by complaining that the "Babylonian queen ... receives the *coup de grâce* from the quadrille manufacturers."[120]

Music was, of course, a prominent feature of the London pleasure gardens during the eighteenth and nineteenth centuries, Vauxhall Gardens in particular, which played Handel's music more frequently when he was alive than that of any other composer. And in this instance, the iconic Handel was literally placed

---

[117] A facsimile of this program can be found in Wollenberg, *Music at Oxford in the Eighteenth and Nineteenth Centuries*, p. 163. The other composers listed on the program were Graun, Beethoven, Stafford Smith, Haydn, Callcott, Bishop, Greville, Romberg, and Mozart.

[118] See Weber, *The Rise of Musical Classics*, p. 174, and Table 3, pp. 249–250.

[119] The "arrangement-industry" created a great deal of work, and profit, in many genres and for many composers, some as well-known as Czerny, Hummel, Moscheles, and even Beethoven.

[120] Eatcock, *Mendelssohn and Victorian England*, p. 14, citing *The Athenaeum*, no. 4 (1828), p. 60. William Parke was equally antagonistic to arrangements, and particularly critical of the version of *Messiah* by no less a composer than Mozart, going so far as to calling it a "posthumous forgery," one "that Mozart [would never] take up his pen for the purpose of depreciating the fame of a great master." See Parke, *Musical Memoirs*, pp. 75–76.

Figure 1 Statue of Handel by Louis François Roubiliac, 1738, Vauxhall
Gardens, now housed at the Victoria and Albert Museum London. Credit: Used
with permission from the Victoria and Albert Museum, London.

on a pedestal, in the shape of an ornate and flattering statue (Figure 1) made by
Louis François Roubiliac (1702–62). It was unveiled on May 1, 1738, and
became the visual centerpiece of the Vauxhall grounds for decades to come.[121]

The atmosphere at Vauxhall seems to have been a curious mixture of music
festival, social hall, gambling center, eating establishment, and amusement
park. It was certainly relaxed and informal, as the conservative John Marsh
commented in his diary after a visit there in 1770: "it was fashion only to attend
to the songs & to walk about during the performance of the instrumental
music."[122] The food was a special feature, but the proprietor and director

---

[121] David Coke and Alan Borg, *Vauxhall Gardens: A History* (New Haven: Yale University Press,
2011), pp. 89–96.
[122] *The John Marsh Journals*, p. 77.

Jonathan Tyer found every possible opportunity to save money, such as offering slices of meat that were so thin that they were dubbed "cobweb sandwiches." This aspect of Tyer's "frugality" with the food at the Gardens soon became so well known throughout London that people who wanted a small portion of meat were reported to ask that it be carved "Vauxhally."[123]

Nevertheless, music was indeed a centerpiece of Vauxhall Gardens, but although Handel dominated at the outset, his star gradually diminished there as it did in the rest of Britain. Haydn was a particularly strong competitor for the public's attention. By 1791, for example, the programs featured sixty-five works by Haydn and only thirty-five by Handel; between 1803 and 1804 the numbers for each were less – but the twenty-six by Haydn were still greater than the sixteen by Handel.[124] A program from May 25, 1793, was typical. It featured an "Overture" to "Samson" by Handel, a written annotation claiming that it "was well received as usual," and a "Full Overture" by "Dr. Haydn," presumably one of his symphonies. The same is true for the concert of June 26, 1793, that listed an "Ov—Bach" (presumably Johann Christian), a "Sym—Haydn," and an "Ov: & Dead March Saul" by Handel.[125]

Haydn himself visited Vauxhall in 1792, marveling on June 4 that "the place and its diversions have no equal in the world." He described "155 dining booths scattered about, all very nice and each comfortably seating six persons," and commented on the low cost of coffee and milk. He did mention that "the music is fairly good," and of course remarked: "a stone statue of Handel is to be seen."[126] The history of that statue, however, symbolically reflects the declining importance of Handel's music after he died. From about 1748 it stood out in the open in the center of the Handel Piazza, but by 1762, it was placed under cover in a simple Doric portico, where it remained until the Vauxhall Jubilee celebrations of 1786. It was moved several more times after that, then sold to a number of individuals, and finally purchased by the Sacred Harmonic Society in 1854 for only 100 guineas. However, the royal family would once again come to Handel's rescue a century later, at least in spirit, when the statue was purchased from Novello and Company Ltd. in 1965 for £10,000 by the Victoria and Albert Museum in London.[127]

---

[123] See Coke and Borg, *Vauxhall Gardens*, p. 198.

[124] See Ian Taylor, *Music in London and the Myth of Decline* (Cambridge: Cambridge University Press, 2010), pp. 91 and 93.

[125] See Coke and Borg, *Vauxhall Gardens*, pp. 170 and 172, respectively.

[126] Coke and Borg, *Vauxhall Gardens*, p. 252.

[127] See Coke and Borg, *Vauxhall Gardens*, p. 95 and the website of the Victoria and Albert Museum: https://collections.vam.ac.uk/item/O34256/georg-frederick-handel-statue-roubiliac-louis-françois/georg-frederick-handel-statue-roubiliac-louis-françois.

Indeed, as noted previously, the British Royal Family played an important role in the promotion of Handel's music, King George III in particular, who reportedly "generally directs [the orchestra] what pieces of music to play, chiefly Handel."[128] Concerts of Handel's music were of such seeming necessity to the King that he insisted that one be held even in the evening of the day on which an attempt was made on his life. However, as McVeigh observes, "for courtiers, on the other hand, attendance was something of a chore."[129] Handel's music remains of great importance to the British royalty, a prime example being that *Zadok the Priest* is performed to this day for royal coronations.

Handel's works were also used for pedagogical purposes throughout the period. Muzio Clementi, who, as we have seen, did so much for the dissemination of the sonatas of Domenico Scarlatti in Britain with his didactic works, also contributed significantly to making Handel's music well known among pianists and piano students. For example, ten "lessons" in the first edition of Clementi's *Introduction* (1801) feature works by Handel; subsequent issues, editions, and appendices contain fewer, but Handel's music is prominent throughout. Volume 1 of *Clementi's Selection of Practical Harmony for the Organ or Piano Forte*, published on November 23, 1801, contains a "'Fuga a 2' in B minor" by Handel, and Volume 2 (ca. February 20, 1802) includes eleven fugues by the composer, five from the *Suite de Pieces* of 1720.[130] It is also interesting to note that when Clementi was asked to play the piano at a celebratory dinner given in his honor at the Albion Hotel on December 17, 1827, the seventy-five-year-old pianist "extemporized on a theme from Handel, and completely carried us away by his fine playing," according to Moscheles, one of the cosponsors of the event.[131]

The music of Handel also found its way into teaching manuals for non-keyboard instruments, such as cello methods. For example, Robert Lindley's *Hand-Book for the Violoncello* features two excerpts by Handel: an "Example from the Bass to the

---

[128] McVeigh, *Concert Life in London*, p. 51.

[129] McVeigh, *Concert Life in London*, p. 51. Leopold Mozart described one such evening, when the eight-year-old Wolfgang performed at the palace on May 19, 1764, writing: "he played off everything *prima vista*. He played so splendidly on the King's organ that they all value his organ-playing more highly than his clavier-playing. Then he accompanied the Queen in an aria which she sang . . . and played the most beautiful melody [some airs of Handel] on it and in such a manner that everyone was amazed." McVeigh notes that Leopold "was even more pleased to receive 24 guineas in cash," reminding us once again of our discussion in the Introduction about the important role of money for foreign visitors to Britain.

[130] See Daw, "Muzio Clementi as an Original Advocate, Collector and Performer," pp. 63–67 for a complete list, and Rosenblum, *Introduction*, pp. xxi–xxxix.

[131] For details, see Planting, *Clementi*, pp. 246–247, and Moscheles, *RMM*, pp. 127–128. According to a report about this dinner in *The Harmonicon*, Moscheles and J. B. Cramer also played "Clementi's duet in E flat, opera 14, with such exquisite skill as renders it impossible to give it due praise." See *The Harmonicon*, January 1828, vol. VI, no. 1, pp. 18–19.

Example 12 Robert Lindley, "Example from the Bass to the 'Minuet in Samson,'" *Hand-Book for the Violoncello*

Example 13 Robert Lindley, "The Harmonious Blacksmith," *Hand-Book for the Violoncello*

'Minuet in Samson'" (see Ex. 12) and an excerpt from "The Harmonious Blacksmith" (see Ex. 13).[132] Handel's "Ye Sacred Priests" and an unnamed Handel excerpt are used by John Gunn in *The Theory and Practice of Fingering the Violoncello: The Second Edition*, and "Handels Gavot [sic]" appears in Robert Crome's *The Compleat Tutor for the Violoncello* (see Ex. 14).[133]

Felix Mendelssohn was a strong advocate for the music of Handel as he would be for that of Bach. It is also fair to say that Handel's oratorios exerted as powerful an influence on Mendelssohn's own works in the genre as they had for Haydn forty years earlier, after he had heard his first live Handel oratorios in London in 1791. Haydn's *Creation* would be inconceivable without his experience with Handel, and the same can be said of Mendelssohn's vocal works, such as the *Te Deum* in D major, MWV B15; *St. Paul*, op. 36; and perhaps most significantly, *Elijah*, op. 70.[134]

Mendelssohn also served Handel well as an organist, and would often try to include a work by Handel in his performances, usually in the form of an improvisation. Such was the case at a Sons of Clergy concert at St Paul's Cathedral on June 25, 1833, when he improvised on themes from Handel's *Dettingen Te Deum* and *Messiah*; he did the same on themes from Handel's

---

[132] Robert Lindley, *Handbook for the Violoncello* (London: Musical Bouquet Office, 1851–1855). The "Minuet in Samson" appears on p. 12, and "The Harmonious Blacksmith" on p. 22.

[133] Robert Crome, *The Compleat Tutor for the Violoncello* (London: C. and S. Thompson, ca. 1765): the "Gavot" appears on p. 29. In John Gunn, *The Theory and Practice of Fingering the Violoncello* (London: the author, 1st ed., 1789), the excerpts are no. 85 (p. 54) and no. 98 (p. 62).

[134] See Larry Todd, *Mendelssohn: A Life in Music* (Oxford: Oxford University Press, 2003), passim, and specifically pp. 152, 157, 159, 185, 337, 381, and 548.

Example 14 Robert Crome, "Handels Gavot [sic]," *The Compleat Tutor for the Violoncello*

Solomon when he conducted his own *Midsummer Night's Dream* overture at the Birmingham Festival on September 19, 1837. Mendelssohn interpolated Bach's *Prelude and Fugue in A Minor* (BWV 543) on the Birmingham Town Hall organ between two choruses from *Israel in Egypt* on September 22, 1840, improvised on themes from Handel's *Jeptha* on the organ three days later, and on June 17, 1842, he did the same at Exeter Hall on Handel's *Harmonious Blacksmith* for the Sacred Harmony Society.[135]

Moscheles also contributed his fair share to promoting Handel's music, not as a conductor or organist, but as a pianist, and on a few occasions, a harpsichordist. The number and variety of keyboard works by Handel that Moscheles played is extensive (see Appendix 2 for a complete list).[136] He also made further forays into the keyboard world of Handel by composing two works in his honor, his *Variations on a Theme of Handel*, op. 29, for solo piano, and the *Hommage à Handel*, op. 92, for two pianos. Moscheles played the *Hommage* most frequently with Mendelssohn, including two concerts in Leipzig in 1835 and 1836 that earned the acclaim of Robert Schumann, who wrote: "I said then that they played together as two eagles. I can also say, they played like the incarnate grandsons of the Handel family."[137] The *Hommage* would go on to become a standard part of the duo-piano repertoire for the next fifty years, appearing on the programs of pianists such as Franz Liszt, William Sterndale Bennett, Julius Benedict, Clara Schumann,

---

[135] See Appendix B, visits I–X, in Eatcock, *Mendelssohn and Victorian England.*

[136] Another indication of Moscheles' great interest in Handel can be found in the list of items from his library auctioned after his death: the works of Handel comprised more than 10 percent of the total volumes. See Kroll, *Ignaz Moscheles*, pp. 306–310 and Mark Kroll, "Moscheles, Handel and the Performance and Reception of Old Music in Nineteenth-Century England," in *Early Music Performer: Journal of the National Early Music Association*, 42 (2018), pp. 17–29, here p. 27.

[137] *Neue Zeitschrift für Musik*, Band IV, No. 46 (Leipzig, June 7, 1836), pp. 191–192.

Arabella Goddard, Sigismond Thalberg, Charles Hallé, Leopold de Meyer, and others. These artists would perform the work either with Moscheles or with each other on their own recitals.[138]

Moscheles also became one of the founding members of the London Handel Society, which his diary tells us was formed in 1842 "for the purpose of publishing an improved edition of Handel's works."[139] Both he and Mendelssohn were appointed as editors of separate volumes, Moscheles for *L'Allegro, Il Penseroso ed Il Moderato* and Mendelssohn for *Israel in Egypt*.[140] Mendelssohn had been asked to make the edition of *Messiah*, but refused because "he felt scruples on account of Mozart's additional accompaniments, and therefore the 'Israel in Egypt' was offered to him instead."[141] He was equally uncompromising in his editing principles, describing the addition of anything that was not Handel's without clearly indicating such changes as editorial to be "no slight evil."[142] This is in contrast to many editors of the period who, with the best of intentions, made alterations and additions to the musical text. Mendelssohn here was thus in agreement with a number of his British contemporaries who were taking gradual steps to achieve varying degrees of authenticity and modern scholarship. One such kindred soul was Vincent Novello, who wrote in May 1825 that he wanted his edition to be practical to be sure but was equally "desirous to give each Piece in its original and complete form . . . to give the whole of the Pieces which require Orchestral Accompaniments *exactly as they were intended to be performed by the Composers*."[143]

Handel after 1850

Handel's music therefore fared far better between 1750 and 1850 than did Scarlatti's, even if most of the performances were excerpts. The same can be

---

[138] For more information, see Kroll, *Ignaz Moscheles*, pp. 277–278, and Kroll, "Moscheles, Handel and the Performance and Reception of Old Music," pp. 17–20. For a comprehensive study of Moscheles' lifelong engagement with the music of Handel, from his early training in Prague until his death in 1870, see Werner Rackwitz, "Ignaz Moscheles – sein Verhältnis zur Musik Georg Friedrich Händel," in *Göttinger Händel-Beiträge*, vol. 13 (2012), pp. 219–243.

[139] Moscheles, *RMM*, p. 291, and Kroll, *Ignaz Moscheles*, p. 279.

[140] Moscheles, *RMM*, pp. 295–296. For Moscheles' approach to editing *L'Allegro*, see Kroll, *Ignaz Moscheles*, pp. 279–284.

[141] Moscheles, *RMM*, p. 299, and Kroll, *Ignaz Moscheles*, p. 279. Clearly Mendelssohn's opinion of Mozart's arrangement was different than Parke's.

[142] He details his objections in a letter to Moscheles of March 7, 1845. See Felix Moscheles, *Letters of Mendelssohn to Moscheles*, pp. 251–252. For further information on the role of Mendelssohn as editor of early music, see Großmann-Vendrey, *Felix Mendelssohn und die Musik der Vergangenheit*, pp. 192–196, and William A. Little, *Mendelssohn and the Organ* (Oxford: Oxford University Press, 2010), pp. 160–165.

[143] Philip Olleson and Fiona M. Palmer, "Publishing Music from the Fitzwilliam Museum," p. 48, citing "The Fitzwilliam Music," signed by Novello (Cu, CUR 30.1, item 60.2).

said of Handel commemorations, which seem to have taken on a life of their own in the nineteenth century, often with no particular reason other than to celebrate Handel's music, as happened in 1857. Handel's iconic stature thus continued relatively unchanged after 1850, and in fact, sometimes got even larger. This was the case with the 1859 festival at the Crystal Palace, which was indeed a real commemoration, in this instance the hundredth anniversary of Handel's death. The article titled "The Great Handel Festival at the Crystal Palace of 1859" that appeared in *The Musical Times* confirms this, in florid prose.

The writer first emphasizes Handel's place in the British pantheon of musicians: "Handel's spirit breathes around us, inspiring, and affording an infinite pleasure to thousands upon thousands of musicians ... Handel was a genius for all ages, the love of his works will never die, but will go on increasing daily in strength."[144] Further reference is made to Handel's connection to Britain:

> England was the home of his adoption, and no composer has greater claims upon the British public ... much of his music is wedded to the service of the Established Church of England, and religious fervour is awakened by the strains of his immortal works. It is to Handel that this country owes the introduction of oratorios; and the fame of his operas still lives, even a century after his demise.

The writer then underscores this point by returning to the subject of the article: "The Handel Commemoration at the Crystal Palace must be taken as a grand national ovation to the genius of the great composer, and proof of the hold which his music has obtained upon the hearts of Englishmen."

It should be noted that these comments about Handel's central role in the musical development of England were not new. They had, in fact been expressed almost one hundred years earlier, in 1762, by John Potter, who wrote:

> English music, at this period, is a composition of German and Italian, in conjunction with the old English music: For this agreeable union we are primarily beholden to Mr Handel: He not only laid the foundation, but liv'd long enough to compleat it. So that the *English* music may with justness be called *Handel's* music, and every musician the son of *Handel*; [...]. He has join'd the fullness and majesty of the *German* music, the delicacy and elegance of the *Italian*, to the solidity of the *English*; constituting in the end a magnificence of style superior to any other nation.[145]

---

[144] "The Great Handel Festival at the Crystal Palace," *The Musical Times and Singing Class Circular*, July 1, 1859, vol. 9, no. 197, pp. 75–78 and 83.

[145] John Potter, in his *Observations on the Present State of Music* (1762), cited in Coke and Borg, *Vauxhall Gardens*, p. 145.

In terms of size and repertoire, the 1859 event also followed a pattern similar to that of previous commemorations, the journal telling the readers: "No expense and no pains have been spared to make this performance perfect, and in every respect it has far exceeded anything of the kind which was ever before attempted." It also featured the expected large number of performers and listeners: "A more magnificent spectacle it would be impossible to conceive than the vast orchestra which was assembled, and the whole formed a picture which none will ever forget. The immense area of the great transept was filled with thousands of spectators." The program, moreover, was also as expected, being that it included a mixture of complete performances (i.e., *Messiah*, the *Dettingen Te Deum*, and *Israel in Egypt*) and excerpts (e.g., *Belshazzar's Feast* and *Judas Maccabaeus*). Also not surprising was the attendance of a member of the royal family, in this instance Prince Albert, although without Queen Victoria, who, as we have discussed, had no love for this repertoire.

As mentioned previously, we can never know for certain how these festivals sounded or were experienced by both performers and audience. A faint glimpse, however, can be gotten from a recording of a performance of yet another excerpt, "Moses and the Children of Israel" from *Israel in Egypt*, which took place at the Crystal Palace on June 29, 1888. Conducted by August Manns, it reportedly featured 500 musicians and 4,000 voices performing for an audience of 23,722. The sound of the recording is dismal, almost inaudible, but one does get a sense of the slow tempo that was necessary in coordinating such large performing forces in a cavernous space.[146]

Handel's keyboard music was also performed with a modest degree of frequency after 1850. Alexandre Billet, for example, played Handel's "Allegro and Fugue in F" on a "Concert of Classical Pianoforte Music" in St. Martin's Hall, March 20, 1852.[147] Handel also appeared on Ernst Pauer's series of historical recitals mentioned in the previous section (e.g., a "suite de pièces" by Handel in 1867), and on Florence May's program of 1886; even Anton Rubinstein, one of the "giant" Romantic pianists of the later nineteenth century, included Handel on his historical recitals that he presented between 1885 and 1886.[148] The Royal Philharmonic also tried its hand at some of Handel's instrumental music, performing a "Concerto grosso in G minor" on May 8, 1871; a "Concerto with Hautboy" on April 15, 1872; the "Concerto

---

[146] The link to this performance is www.youtube.com/watch?v=zXWO3JOKLts.

[147] Ritterman and Weber, "Origins of the Piano Recital in England, 1830–1870," p. 181.

[148] De Val and Ehrlich, "Repertory and Canon," in *The Cambridge Companion to the Piano*, pp. 129–130. Rubinstein's recitals were chronological programs that began with English virginalists, and continued with the French *clavecinistes*, Bach, Handel, C. P. E. Bach and later composers.

Grosso, No. 11, in A" on March 25, 1874; and an "Overture" on March 12, 1885 (see Appendix 1).

Nevertheless, despite any criticisms one might level at the Philharmonic, or for that matter most musicians and audiences in Britain, Handel's music was treated quite well between 1750 and 1850 and afterwards. As we have seen, the same cannot be said for Scarlatti's, and the situation was equally disappointing with regards to the music of J. S. Bach, which we discuss in the next section.

4 Johann Sebastian Bach

The critic F. G. Edwards, in his retrospective essay of 1896 "Bach's Music in England," uses the word "vile" to describe the performance of the duet and chorus "My Saviour Jesus now is taken" from the Saint Matthew Passion at the Birmingham Festival of 1837.[149] Could it really have been that bad? Apparently so, and things did not seem to improve much a year later, when the *Gloria, Qui sedes*, and *Quoniam tu solus* of Bach's B-minor Mass were performed on May 23, 1838, at the "Antient Concert." Citing *The Musical World* from that time, Edwards reports that the overall performance was "execrable." The trumpet player "Mr. Harper" could not play his part in the *Gloria* because he did not have the correct instrument; the oboist Grattan Cooke "stopped at the very outset of his exertions" with the aria *Qui sedes* because the "obligato accompaniment [was written] for the tenoroon or oboe d'amore," neither of which Cooke had; and the *Quoniam tu solus* was "slaughtered" because the bassoon part "appeared greatly incorrect." This resulted in "the soli players retiring in dismay, and leaving Mr. Knyvett to play their parts on the organ, which he did most manfully."[150]

These are admittedly extreme examples, but as discussed earlier, the music of J. S. Bach was the slowest to be accepted by British performers and audiences between 1750 and 1850. Domenico Scarlatti had his early advocates, such as Roseingrave, Kelway, and Avison, and somewhat later, Worgan and Clementi. Handel had the entire British nation on his side during his lifetime and after his death. J. S. Bach, however, the member of this triumvirate who now inspires unanimous worldwide reverence today, was the last to be fully recognized and accepted by British music lovers. What might have caused this resistance, or at least its delay? The British public could certainly not be accused of shunning large-scale choral works; their love of Handel's massive oratorios, even when only given in excerpts, proves otherwise. Virtuoso keyboard music also posed

---

[149] F. G. Edwards, "Bach's Music in England," *The Musical Times and Singing Class Circular*, vol. 37, no. 645 (November 1, 1896), pp. 722–726, here p. 725.

[150] F. G. Edwards, "Bach's Music in England," p. 725.

no obstacle. Although the technical demands of Bach's keyboard works are formidable, generations of British musicians who were comfortable with the challenging keyboard works from the Elizabethan period, such as John Bull's "Walsingham," and could also play and enjoy the eighteenth-century harpsichordist William Babell's virtuoso keyboard arrangements of Handel opera arias, would probably not be intimidated by many of J. S. Bach's keyboard works. Negotiating Scarlatti's harpsichord sonatas was also no mean accomplishment, even in Pittman's simplified versions.

The German language of many of Bach's vocal works also should not have been a problem. The British had little difficulty listening to or singing in other languages, such as Italian or Latin, and it should not be forgotten that the Georgian courts that dominated British history during this period were essentially German-speaking, thus providing a comfortable environment in which Continental musicians from the German-speaking lands could live and work. Handel is a prime example. Johann Christian Bach, Queen Charlotte's music master, is another.[151] As mentioned, this Germanic tradition continued with Prince Albert (himself a member of the German nobility) and through Queen Victoria's reign, until World War I forced the royal family to make a discreet political change of their name from Hanover to Windsor.[152]

Nevertheless, it is an uncontestable fact that it took until the final decades of the eighteenth century before the music of Johann Sebastian Bach began to make inroads into British musical taste. One of the possible reasons for this surprising development might be traced to Charles Burney, who seized almost every opportunity to disparage J. S. Bach's music and compare it unfavorably to that of Handel. And this despite the fact that Burney apparently received his first substantial exposure to the works of J. S. Bach from no less an authoritative source than Bach's own son, Carl Philipp Emanuel, whom Burney visited in Hamburg in October 1772. As Burney writes: "Mr Bach shewed me two manuscript books of his father's composition, written on purpose for him when he was a boy, containing pieces with a fugue, in all the twenty-four keys, extremely difficult, and generally in five parts, at which he laboured for the first years of his life, without remission."[153]

---

[151] Andrew Hyatt King observes that among the Royal Library's collection of music by Johann Christian Bach are eight of his major works in autograph, "some of which bear the words: 'This volume belongs to the Queen, 1788.'" See Andrew Hyatt King, "English Royal Music-Lovers and Their Library, 1600–1900," *The Musical Times*, vol. 99, no. 1384 (June 1958), pp. 311–313, here p. 312.

[152] A notable example was Lord Mountbatten, a leading member of the House of Windsor, whose ancestral name was Battenberg.

[153] Charles Burney, *The Present State of Music in Germany, the Netherlands, and United Provinces* (London: T. Becket & Co., 1773), vol. 2, p. 272, cited in *The English Bach Awakening: Knowledge of J. S. Bach and His Music in England 1750–1830*, ed. Michael Kassler

Indeed, Burney rarely failed to tell his British readers that J. S. Bach's music was "extremely difficult," criticism that he would repeat frequently in his writings about the composer, and not without some justification. Bach's keyboard music is certainly less accessible and playable than that of Handel, who did not devote much energy or attention to this genre throughout his career. British musicians were also more hesitant to adopt Bach's music with the same enthusiasm as for that of Domenico Scarlatti, at least at the outset, whose harpsichord sonatas, challenging as they might be, usually maintained a predominantly two-voice texture that did not approach the complexity of a five-voice fugue by Bach.

Another striking feature of Burney's report from Hamburg is his description of seeing pieces "in all the twenty-four keys." This is most certainly a reference to J. S. Bach's *The Well-Tempered Clavier*. But Burney also writes that there were "two manuscript books." Does this mean that C. P. E. Bach had manuscript copies of *both* Books I *and* II of *The Well-Tempered Clavier* in Hamburg, and that he gave away, to someone he had never previously met, and an Englishman no less, not one but two precious manuscript copies of his father's most famous keyboard compositions? We will probably never have a definitive answer to these questions, although the evidence points in other directions, at least for Book II.[154]

Despite Carl Philipp Emanuel's kindness and generosity, however, Burney's attitude to the music of J. S. Bach did not improve after his visit in 1772. In fact, his criticism became even harsher, especially when he was comparing Bach's music to Handel's. For example, in 1789, a year after the death of his host in Hamburg, Burney launched into another diatribe about Carl Philipp Emanuel's father, exclaiming: "Handel was perhaps the only great Fughuist [sic], exempt from pedantry" because his themes, rather than being "barren or crude," were "almost always natural and pleasing." For Burney, Bach's fugal themes were never "natural and *chantant*," nor was there ever "an easy and obvious passage,

(Aldershot: Ashgate, 2004), "Chronology," p. 5; and Yo Tomita, "'Most ingenious, most learned, and yet practicable work': The English Reception of Bach's *Well-Tempered Clavier* in the First Half of the Nineteenth Century seen through the Editions Published in London," in Ellsworth and Wollenberg, eds., *The Piano in Nineteenth-Century British Culture*, pp. 33–67, here p. 34.

[154] I am grateful to Robert Marshall for his insights and suggestions about this matter, and for his references to the Critical Reports of Alfred Durr in his edition of Books I and II. See Johann Sebastian Bach, *Neue Ausgabe Sämtliche Werke, Serie V, Band 6.1* (Kassel: Bärenreiter, 1989), pp. 116–117, and *Serie V, Band 6.2* (Kassel: Bärenreiter, 1996), p. 21. For further discussion about these and other questions relating to the history of *The Well-Tempered Clavier* in Britain, see Yo Tomita, "The Dawn of the English Bach Awakening Manifested in Sources of the '48'" in Kassler, *The English Bach Awakening*, pp. 35–167. His discussions about Charles Burney can be found on pp. 49–64.

that is not loaded with crude and difficult accompaniments."[155] Burney would nevertheless have to acknowledge that Handel and Bach "are the most renowned organists of the eighteenth century," and cited the *Credo* from Bach's B-minor mass as "one of the most clear, correct, and masterly" settings that he had ever seen.[156]

Burney, furthermore, was of the opinion that Bach was only a composer of "learned music" that was rarely pleasant to listen to, explaining: "A long & laboured Fugue, *recte et retro* in 40 parts, may be a good Entertainment for the *Eyes* of a Critic, but can never delight the *Ears* of a Man of Taste."[157] The difficulty of Bach's keyboard music was another target of Burney's criticism, even though, as I have mentioned, British pianists were already familiar with challenging works. Burney, however, even expressed this reservation when praising the remarkable performance of Bach by a young prodigy, Godfrey William Palschau (ca. 1744–1815). In a talk Burney gave to the "Royal Society of London" on February 18, 1779, he recalled hearing "PALSCHAU, a German boy of nine or ten years old, then in London, perform with great accuracy many of the most difficult compositions that have ever been written for keyed instruments [e.g., Bach's 'lessons and double fugues']," noting that "at that time there were very few masters in Europe able to execute these difficult works."[158]

Burney's recollections about the Palschau concert, however, do tell us that at least some of Bach's keyboard works were available and heard in Britain as early as the middle of the eighteenth century, since he referred to hearing the prodigy play "about thirty years ago," meaning around 1749.[159] The brief biography of Bach that appeared in a *General History of the Science and Practice of Music*, published by John Hawkins in 1776, is another indication that Bach and his music were not entirely unknown in the British Isles around this time.[160] J. S. Bach's

---

[155] Burney, *A General History of Music*, p. 96. See also Tomita, in Kassler, *The Dawn of the English Bach Awakening*, p. 57. Never one to pull his punches, Burney had similarly harsh words about another great, non-British keyboard composer, François Couperin, criticizing his *pièces de clavecin* for being too "crowded and deformed by beats, trills, shakes." Charles Burney, *A General History of Music*, p. 996.

[156] Burney, *A General History of Music*, pp. 952–953. See also Kassler, *The English Bach Awakening*, "Chronology," p. 10.

[157] Tomita, in Kassler, *The Dawn of the English Bach Awakening*, p. 50.

[158] Tomita, in Kassler, *The Dawn of the English Bach Awakening*, pp. 37 and 55, citing Charles Burney, "Account of an Infant Musician," *Philosophical Transactions of the Royal Society of London*, vol. 69 (1779), p. 202.

[159] The actual date of Palschau's performance was 1754, as advertised in *The Public Advertiser*, no. 5994, of January 12, 1754. As Tomita points out, a large number of Bach manuscripts "were disseminated . . . by professional dealers [and some] reached England through various channels, perhaps even in Bach's lifetime." See Tomita, in Kassler, *The Dawn of the English Bach Awakening*, p. 37.

[160] Sir John Hawkins, *A General History of the Science and Practice of Music* (London: T. Payne and Son, 1776). The biography, plus the Aria and Variations 9 and 10 from the *Goldberg*

Example 15 J. S. Bach, *Partita in B-Flat Major*, BWV 825, movement
I, mm. 1–4

Partita in B-Flat Major, BWV 825 (see Ex. 15), or at least part of it, had also been heard in England during this period, although most listeners were probably not aware they were doing so. The opening passage of the first sonata in Johann Christian Bach's *Six Sonatas for the Harpsichord or Pianoforte with an Accompaniment for a Violin*, op. 10 (published 1773; see Ex. 16) is a direct quote, albeit simplified and rhythmically altered, from the first measures of his father's *Partita*.

It is also possible that J. C. Bach may have been responsible for the addition of a manuscript containing Books I and II of *The Well-Tempered Clavier* and Part III of J. S. Bach's *Clavierübung* to the library of his employer, Queen Charlotte.[161]

Bach's place in the pantheon of musicians in Britain was thus not to be denied, and his stature would be considerably enhanced with the arrival of a group of the Bach-loving German-speaking immigrants mentioned in the Introduction who came to England during the final decades of the eighteenth century. In a certain sense, these pioneers created a Bach "sect" of their own, not in name but certainly in spirit, that would rival and surpass in size and impact that of Scarlatti advocates such as Roseingrave, Kelway, Avison, and Worgan.

Variations (BWV 988), appears on pp. 852–855. See Kassler, *The English Bach Awakening*, "Chronology," p. 6.

[161] The source for this information comes from Kassler, *The English Bach Awakening*, "Chronology," p. 8 and A. Hyatt King, *Some British Collectors of Music*, Appendix A. Kassler writes that this is according to "Queen Charlotte's principal page Frederick Nicolay (ca.1728–1809), who was responsible for the royal music library, and annotated the Queen's music collection at this time." The manuscript is now BL R.M. 21.a.9.

Example 16 Johann Christian Bach, *Six Sonatas for the Harpsichord or Pianoforte with an Accompaniment for a Violin*, op. 10, movement I, mm. 1–5

One of the earliest members of the "Bach squad," as it is sometimes called, was Augustus Frederic Christopher Kollmann (1756–1829), dubbed by Yo Tomita and others as "The First Apostle of Bach in England."[162] He arrived in London in 1782, the same year as Charles Frederick Horn (1756–1829), and this honorific title is not without some justification. Kollmann's *An Essay on Practical Musical Composition* (1799), featured or quoted from numerous compositions by Bach, such as the *Trio Sonata for Organ in E-Flat Major* (BWV 525); the *Prelude and Fugue in C Major* (BWV 870) from Book II of *The Well-Tempered Clavier*; and portions of the *Musical Offering* (BWV 1079), *The Art of Fugue* (BWV 1080), *Chromatic Fantasy and Fugue* (BWV 903), and other works.[163] More significantly, Kollmann subsequently collaborated with Horn, who had become Queen Charlotte's new music master after J. C. Bach's

---

[162] See Yo Tomita, "'Most ingenious, most learned, and yet practicable work': The English Reception of Bach's *Well-Tempered Clavier* in the First Half of the Nineteenth Century seen through the Editions Published in London," p. 35. For a full discussion of Kollman's contributions, see Tomita, in Kassler, *The Dawn of the English Bach Awakening*, p. 112–122. For the work of the other German advocates, see Tomita, "The English Reception of Bach's *Well-Tempered Clavier*," and in Kassler, *The Dawn of the English Bach Awakening*, passim.

[163] Tomita writes that Kollman's edition "was the first publication of BWV 525 and BWV 870 anywhere." Tomita, in Kassler, *The Dawn of the English Bach Awakening*, p. 114.

death, and supplied him with the manuscript from which Horn and Samuel Wesley would prepare the first complete English edition of *The Well-Tempered Clavier*.[164]

Among the other German-speaking immigrants from this period who contributed to the incipient British Bach revival were Charles Frederick Baumgarten (ca. 1738–1824) and John Casper Heck (d. 1791). The first edition of J. S. Bach's *Fugue in C Major* (BWV 953) appears unnamed in Heck's tutor, *The Art of Playing the Harpsichord* (1770), and Heck later complained in his *The Musical Library & Universal Magazine of Harmony* (ca. 1780) that Bach, although a "truly great master," was "so little known in this country [i.e., Britain]." This article also includes a short life of Bach taken in part from Burney's *Present State of Music in Germany*, a short list of Bach's musical compositions, an incipit from his "Vom Himmel hoch" (BWV 769), and the first printing anywhere of the entire "Contrapunctus 7" from the *The Art of Fugue* (BWV 1080).[165]

Native Britons were soon to eagerly join in this endeavor. James William Windsor (1756–1853), a fine pianist in Bath who had earned the nickname "The Harmonious Blacksmith" because of his frequent and excellent performances of the Handel variations of the same name, was one of the subscribers to Kollmann's *Essay*; two years after its publication, the twenty-five-year-old Windsor made his own copy of both books of *The Well-Tempered Clavier*.[166] In 1798, John Wall Callcott (1766–1821) founded the Concentores Society, mentioned previously. This organization limited its membership to twelve learned professional musicians, each of whom was required to be able to write "correct counterpoint or perform music in the antique style."[167] Other small groups and clubs, also mentioned in the Introduction, encouraged the composition and performance of contrapuntal music, such as canons, catches, and glees. To cite a notable example, the holdings of the Catch Club included a copy of the four-part canon BWV 1074 entitled "Canone Enimmatico/ J. S. Bach at Leipzig 1725," written in the hand of Edmund Thomas Warren (ca. 1730–1794), secretary of the club from 1761 to 1794, implying that it and other Bach canons were sung at the meetings.[168]

Interest in the music of J. S. Bach seems to have picked up steam by the turn of the century. The first publication anywhere of Bach's *Prelude in D Minor*

---

[164] Bernarr Rainbow, *Four Centuries of Music Teaching Manuals 1518–1932* (Woodbridge: The Boydell Press, 1992), p. 86.

[165] See Kassler, *The English Bach Awakening*, "Chronology," p. 7 and Tomita, in Kassler, *The Dawn of the English Bach Awakening*, pp. 65–66.

[166] See Kassler, *The English Bach Awakening*, "Chronology," p. 13.

[167] Tomita, in Kassler, *The Dawn of the English Bach Awakening*, p. 68.

[168] Tomita, in Kassler, *The Dawn of the English Bach Awakening*, p. 63.

from *The Well-Tempered Clavier* I (BWV 851) appeared in William Shield's *An Introduction to Harmony* (published 1800); around 1823, the esteemed London pianist and piano teacher John Baptist Cramer (1771–1858) published a transcription for two violins, viola, violoncello, and double bass of works by Bach, including the D-major fugue from Book II of *The Well-Tempered Clavier* and the *Fantasy in G Major* (BWV 572); and another well-known English pianist, Cipriani Potter (1792–1871), reportedly memorized both books of *The Well-Tempered Clavier* as part of his studies with the composer and pianist Joseph Woeffl.[169]

Muzio Clementi was almost as active in promoting the music of Bach as he was for that of Domenico Scarlatti and Handel. The first publication of the "Polonoise" [sic] from Bach's "French Suite" in E major (BWV 817) appeared in his *Introduction* of 1801, as did the "Minuet" from the same suite (Lesson XLVIII). Volume 1 of *Clementi's Selection of Practical Harmony for the Organ or Piano Forte* (1801) features a "Suite in G" by Bach (BWV 816) and a "Preludio: Gravement" (BWV 572); volume 2 (1802) includes the first complete publication anywhere of the *Toccata in D Minor* (BWV 913); and volume 3 (1811) was devoted exclusively to the music of Bach. It includes fugues (each titled "Fuga") in C minor (BWV 575), A minor (BWV 944), and C major (BWV 953).[170] The "Appendix" to the fifth edition of *Clementi's Introduction to the Art of Playing on the Piano Forte* (1811) reprints the "Polonoise" [sic] and "Minuet" from the first edition.

Clementi also seems to have passed on his admiration for Bach to his pupils, most notably John Field (1782–1837), who in August 1802 reportedly played in Paris "some of the great fugues of Sebastian Bach with such precision and inimitable taste as to call forth, from a Parisian audience, the most enthusiastic applause."[171] Another Clementi pupil, Ludwig Berger, was reported to have "won for himself friends and the approbation of artists and public alike for his pure and expressive playing of Sebastian Bach."[172]

As the pace of British interest in Bach's music increased, so did the number of native Englishmen who became active in the endeavor. Among them was the publisher Thomas Boosey, who made a major contribution with his publication of an English translation of Forkel's biography of Bach in

---

[169] See Kassler, *The English Bach Awakening*, "Chronology," p. 12; Tomita, in Kassler, *The Dawn of the English Bach Awakening*, p. 80, n. 126; and Kassler, *The English Bach Awakening*, "Chronology," p. 15, respectively.

[170] See Daw, "Muzio Clementi as an Original Advocate, Collector and Performer," pp. 63–68, and Kassler, *The English Bach Awakening*, "Chronology," pp. 13–14.

[171] *The Quarterly Musical Magazine and Review*, vol. ii (1820), pp. 312–13, cited in Plantinga, *Clementi*, p. 154. See also Tomita, in Kassler, *The Dawn of the English Bach Awakening*, p. 79.

[172] *Berlinische musikalische Zeitung*, vol. i (1805), p. 366, cited in Plantinga, *Clementi*, p. 202.

1820, as *The Life of John Sebastian Bach; with a Critical View of His Compositions.*[173] William Crotch offered a cogent discussion of Bach's compositional style in his *Substance ... of Lectures on Music* that reflects much of the thinking about Bach and his music in Britain during the first decades of the nineteenth century.[174] Crotch begins by praising the English translation of Forkel's "The Life of John Sebastian Bach" for its "just sentiments and sound principles of criticism," and continues by making a clear distinction between Bach's sacred and secular music, asserting that sacred music should be performed on the organ and secular works on the clavichord. According to Crotch, "Bach, and his son, William Freidemann [sic] [were] elegant performers on the clavichord," so much so that when he heard "William Freidemann [sic] on the clavichord, all was delicate, elegant, agreeable, and pretty." When Crotch heard him on the organ, however, he "was seized with reverential awe. All was grand and solemn. The same was the case with Sebastian Bach in a higher degree."[175] From these experiences, and other analytical and aesthetic principles, Crotch draws the conclusion that the fugues of Bach (i.e., secular music) "were not intended for the organ, [but] were composed for the clavichord."[176]

He goes further, however, by adding that Bach tuned his clavichord "according to the equal temperament, of which also I always declared my preference."[177] Crotch's definitive statement that equal temperament was his tuning system of choice, at least for the music of J. S. Bach, and, one might assume, also for that of Handel, Scarlatti, and other eighteenth-century composers, raises the interesting question of how keyboards were tuned throughout the period 1750–1850, and particularly in the nineteenth century. It is beyond the scope of this Element to address this controversial subject in depth, but the evidence seems to point to the gradual adoption of equal temperament, at least for pianos, during this era, both in Britain and on the European continent.[178]

---

[173] For more information on the English translations of the Forkel biography of Bach, see Michael Kassler, "The English Translations of Forkel's *Life of Bach*," in *The English Bach Awakening*, pp. 169–209.

[174] William Crotch, *Substance of ... Lectures on Music*, pp. 113–120.

[175] William Crotch, *Substance of ... Lectures on Music*, p. 114.

[176] William Crotch, *Substance of ... Lectures on Music*, p. 115.

[177] William Crotch, *Substance of ... Lectures on Music*, pp. 115–116. Crotch refers to "page 7" of his lectures at this point.

[178] A notable example from this era is the endorsement of equal temperament by Johann Nepomuk Hummel, in Part III, Chapter VI of his piano treatise, *A Complete Theoretical & Practical Course of Instructions on the Art of Playing the Piano Forte* (London: T. Boosey, 1828). See the facsimile of Part III of the Boston edition, Mark Kroll, ed. (Hillsdale, NY: Pendragon Press, 2019), pp. 106–109.

Furthermore, in these pages Crotch could also not let pass an opportunity to compare Bach with Handel. Not surprisingly, and reminiscent of Burney's criticisms years earlier, he chooses Handel as the superior composer, using the visual arts as a point of departure: "Bach became the Michael Angelo of our art, as Handel was our Raffaelle," and since "Raffaelle is generally acknowledged to be the greatest of painters . . . Handel may thus be preferred, because his vocal music and choruses are superior to Bach's, and for the vast variety of his excellence." Nevertheless, Bach must be given his due, even by an Englishman, Crotch conceding that "Bach is unrivalled" for the "science and elevation of style (particularly in the composition of fugues), for the power of abstracting the mind from all surrounding objects, and so relieving it from care and sorrow itself." Crotch concludes that "the study of all his works is therefore earnestly recommended."[179]

The most important British performer, scholar, advocate, and editor of Bach's music during this period, however, was Samuel Wesley (1766–1837). Wesley began to publicly promote the music of J. S. Bach early in his career, and performed it at venues such as the Covent Garden Lenten oratorio concerts, where he was appointed the principal organist in January 1813, the Hanover Square Rooms, and after services at the Portuguese Embassy Chapel, where he was assistant to Vincent Novello (1781–1861). One of the most significant of his many contributions to the promotion of Bach's music in Britain was his joint publication of *The Well-Tempered Clavier* with C. F. Horn, the first volume appearing on September 17, 1810.[180]

After this work by the early German-speaking immigrants, the Italian Clementi, and Wesley and his British contemporaries, the cause of Johann Sebastian Bach in Britain was again taken up by a German, Felix Mendelssohn, as well as the Bohemian Ignaz Moscheles. Mendelssohn made his greatest impact with Bach's organ music, an accomplishment that is all the more significant in the context of the state of organ building in Britain at this time, which was far less advanced than it was in Germany or other European countries. In point of fact, until the late eighteenth century few organs in England had pedalboards at all; they were mostly rudimentary "pull downs,"

---

[179] William Crotch, *Substance of . . . Lectures on Music*, pp. 119–120.

[180] There is a large literature about Wesley and his contributions to the performance of Bach in Great Britain. They include the following: Philip Olleson, "Samuel Wesley and the English Bach Awakening," in Kassler, *The English Bach Awakening*, pp. 251–313; Michael Kassler and Philip Olleson, *Samuel Wesley (1766–1837): A Source Book* (Aldershot: Ashgate, 2001); *The Letters of Samuel Wesley: Professional and Social Correspondence, 1797–1837*, ed. Philip Olleson (Oxford: Oxford University Press, 2001); Michael Kassler, "The Bachists of 1810: Subscribers to the Wesley/Horn Edition of the '48,'" in Kassler, *The English Bach Awakening*, pp. 315–340; and many others.

and if a British organ did have an independent pedalboard, its range was limited at best.[181] This forced musicians who wanted to perform the great organ music of Bach, with its virtuoso pedal parts, into uncomfortable compromises. One alternative was to have two or more keyboard players assume the duties of playing the three independent voices, often at two or more pianos. F. G. Edwards describes such a configuration: the *Prelude and Fugue in E-Flat Major*, "St. Anne" (BWV 552) was played "at St. James's Church, Bermondsey, April 23, 1829 ... in a somewhat novel manner-viz., by *three* performers. Two of the players sat at the ordinary keyboards, while the third played the pedal part on a separate *manual* at the side!"[182] Another alternative was to give the pedal part to a string instrument, such as the double bass. This too is described by Edwards: "A Separate part of the Double Bass, or Violoncello, arranged from the Pedals by Signor Dragonetti, is added" to the edition of the "GRAND STUDIES for the organ," published in 1836 by "Messrs. Coventry and Hollier."[183]

Our Bach "Apostle," A. F. C. Kollmann summarized the situation in 1812, writing that the "fine compositions for the organ" published by Wesley "are still for manual keys only, and the use of obligato pedals is not yet promoted by them." Indeed, Kollmann was astonished that there wasn't a single organ in Britain equal to those in Germany or the Netherlands, despite London being "the most opulent city on the face of the globe."[184]

Mendelssohn therefore often had to revert to the two-player approach when he performed Bach's organ music in Britain, as happened during a musical evening at the home of Friedrich Heinke in 1833, when another guest, the pianist Johann Baptist Cramer, played the pedal line while Mendelssohn assumed the responsibility for the keyboard parts in a performance of two organ works by Bach.[185] Fortunately, Mendelssohn was able to find instruments with a sufficient pedalboard often enough to be able to give complete organ performances of Bach that might come close to the composer's intentions, an important philosophy of his, as we have seen in his approach to editing *Israel in Egypt*. One of Mendelssohn's favorite churches for this

---

[181] See Philip Olleson, "Samuel Wesley and the Development of the Organ Pedals in England," in *Music and Performance Culture in Nineteenth-Century Britain: Essays in Honour of Nicholas Temperley*, ed. Bennett Zon (Surrey: Ashgate, 2012), pp. 283–297.

[182] F. G. Edwards, "Bach's Music in England," p. 723.

[183] F. G. Edwards, "Bach's Music in England," p. 724.

[184] Andrew McCrea, "British organ music after 1800," in *The Cambridge Companion to the Organ*, ed. Nicholas Thistlethwaite and Geoffrey Webber (Cambridge: Cambridge University Press, 1998), p. 279, citing A. F. C. Kollmann, *The Quarterly Musical Register*, January 1, 1812, pp. 15 and 21.

[185] Russell Stinson, *The Reception of Bach's Organ Works from Mendelssohn to Brahms* (Oxford: Oxford University Press, 2006), p. 37.

purpose was St. Paul's Cathedral, since its three-manual organ by Bernard Smith was one of the few instruments in the city at this time with a two-octave pedalboard (C-c^1). There, on June 10, 1832, Mendelssohn is reported to have played "fugue music … to the amazement of all the listeners," and to have "excited so much attention by his treatment of the pedal-board that a complete revolution in the style of English organ-playing may be dated from that memorable performance."[186]

Indeed, Mendelssohn did have a number of chances to display his foot-work to full advantage during his visits to England. One occurred on September 22, 1837, when he performed Bach's *Prelude and Fugue in E-Flat Major* (BWV 552) on the Hill organ of the Birmingham Town Hall.[187] As mentioned in Section 3 on Handel, Mendelssohn would perform on that organ again on September 22, 1840, interpolating Bach's *Prelude and Fugue in A Minor* (BWV 543) between two choruses from *Israel in Egypt*.[188]

Mendelssohn also found the opportunity to meet the legendary Bach advocate Samuel Wesley himself during one of his organ-playing appearances in London. The meeting was apparently so memorable and touching that Mendelssohn described it twice, the first time in his diary:

> At one o'clock I had to go to Christ Church to play the organ. The whole church, choir and everywhere, was stuffed full of people … Old Wesley, trembling and bent, shook hands with me and at my request sat down at the organ bench to play, a thing he had not done for many years. The frail old man improvised with great artistry and splendid facility, so that I could not but admire. His daughter was so moved by the sight of it all that she fainted and could not stop crying and sobbing. She believed she would certainly never hear him play like that again; and alas, shortly after my return to Germany I learned of his death.[189]

He later shared the experience with his wife Cécile:

> I wrote to you early in the morning, and then went to play the organ. There were I suppose about a thousand people gathered together there, the church packed full. I could hardly push my way through to the organ bench, and there sat a 78-year-old organist, the most famous one here, Wesley, who though old and weak, had had himself brought there by his daughters, and at my request he sat himself at the organ bench and played, and it was so moving that his

---

[186] See Stinson, *The Reception of Bach's Organ Works*, p. 29.

[187] Stinson, *The Reception of Bach's Organ Works*, p. 47.

[188] Eatcock, *Mendelssohn and Victorian England*, pp. 71–72. For a complete list of Bach organ works performed by Mendelssohn during his visits to England, see Stinson, *The Reception of Bach's Organ Works*, pp. 73–74.

[189] Stinson, *The Reception of Bach's Organ Works*, p. 45.

daughter burst into the bitterest tears and had to be led down into the sacristy.[190]

Mendelssohn also gave performances of Bach as a pianist during his visits to England, often as a member of a trio playing a Bach triple keyboard concerto. One notable example occurred on June 1, 1844, where he joined Moscheles and Sigismond Thalberg in Bach's *Triple Concerto in D Minor* (BWV 1063).[191] Charles Horsley, writing after almost thirty years, vividly recalled Mendelssohn's cadenza during this performance:

> It began very quietly and the themes of the concerto, most scientifically varied, gradually crept up in their new garments. A crescendo then began ... and at last a storm, nay a perfect hurricane of octaves which must have lasted five minutes, brought to a conclusion an exhibition of mechanical skill, and the most perfect inspiration, which neither before nor since that memorable Thursday afternoon has ever been approached.[192]

Mendelssohn also took up the baton for Bach on at least one occasion during his visits to England, conducting the premiere of Bach's *Orchestral Suite No. 3 in D Major* (BWV 1068) on June 24, 1844 at the penultimate Philharmonic concert of the season at the Hanover Square Rooms.[193]

Ignaz Moscheles also shared his close friend's passion for Bach's music. In fact, his diaries reveal that his longstanding interest in Bach was stimulated by his first encounter with the Mendelssohn family in Berlin in 1824, writing that Mendelssohn's "elder sister Fanny" was "extraordinarily gifted, played by heart, and with admirable precision, Fugues and Passacailles by Bach." Bach continued to be performed and heard in connection with the Mendelssohns throughout Moscheles' 1824 visit. The diary tells us that on November 23 "the brother and sister played Bach"; we read that on November 28 Moscheles heard a "concerto by Bach" at the Mendelssohn house; and the entry of December 3 tells us that at the "Music at Zelter's" Fanny Mendelssohn played "the D minor Concerto by S. Bach [i.e., the *Concerto for Harpsichord in D Minor*, BWV 1052] which I saw in the original manuscript."[194]

From that visit on, Moscheles' thirst for the music of Bach became "simply unquenchable," as he described to Mendelssohn in a letter of August 14,

---

[190] Stinson, *The Reception of Bach's Organ Works*, p. 45 and p. 189, n. 135.

[191] For information about this concert and the overall relationship between Moscheles and Mendelssohn, see Kroll, *Ignaz Moscheles*, chapter 6 and passim.

[192] Charles Edward Horsley, "Reminiscences of Mendelssohn by His English Pupil," in *Dwight's Journal of Music*, January 11, 1873, 32/20, cited in Eatcock, *Mendelssohn and Victorian England*, p. 86. For further information on Mendelssohn's performance of the Bach keyboard concerto and others, see Kroll, *Ignaz Moscheles*, p. 268.

[193] Eatcock, *Mendelssohn and Victorian England*, p. 87.

[194] Moscheles, *RMM*, p. 65, and Kroll, *Ignaz Moscheles*, p. 264.

1836.[195] Since Moscheles was not an organist, he satisfied that thirst by performing as many of Bach's harpsichord works as he could (on the piano), such as the *Chromatic Fantasy and Fugue* (BWV 903) and numerous preludes from *The Well-Tempered Clavier*, Books I and II, not to mention a *Ricercare* (either three-part or six-part) from the *Musical Offering* (BWV 1079); the *Toccata in E Minor* (BWV 914); and multiple harpsichord concertos, including a rarity, the *Concerto for Harpsichord and Two Recorders in F Major* (BWV 1057), which is Bach's arrangement of his *Brandenburg Concerto No. 4 in G Major* (BWV 1049). (See Appendix 3 for a complete list of keyboard works by Bach that Moscheles performed during his career.) Moscheles and Fétis also included a work by Bach in their *Méthode des Méthodes*, as they had done for Scarlatti: Bach's *Prelude and Fugue in D Minor* (BWV 851) from *The Well-Tempered Clavier*, Book I.[196] Interestingly, there is no example by Handel in the *Méthode*, which is perhaps a comment on the perceived relative unimportance of his keyboard works as compared to those of Scarlatti and Bach. Finally, as he did for Handel by founding and joining the London Handel Society, Moscheles became a founding member of the *Bach Gesellschaft* in Leipzig after moving to that city in 1846.[197]

Nevertheless, Moscheles felt as little compunction in tampering with the music of J. S. Bach (one of his musical gods, just below Beethoven) as he and his colleagues did with that of Handel. To cite a notable example, Moscheles added woodwind instruments to Bach's original string ensemble for a performance of the *Concerto for Harpsichord in D Minor* (BWV 1052) on May 11, 1836, an innovation that met with the full approval of *The Musical World*: "The orchestral accompaniments were re-scored for the occasion by Mr. Moscheles, and the wind instrument parts (the whole written in masterly keeping with the genius and character of the music) were entirely by Mr. Moscheles."[198] *The Atlas* also seems to have applauded, or at least did not object to, the "additional accompaniments for the orchestra."[199] Moscheles himself proudly explained how and why he had reorchestrated Bach in his letter to Mendelssohn of August 14, 1836: "You ask me about my scoring of the Bach Concerto. Well, it seemed to me that one might give it a kind of new varnish, by doing for it what Mozart had done with such perfect taste for the 'Messiah,' when he added wind-instruments to the score." We also learn here exactly what

---

[195] Felix Moscheles, ed., *Letters of Felix Mendelssohn to Ignaz and Charlotte Moscheles*, p. 153.
[196] Fétis and Moscheles, *Méthode des Méthodes*, pp. 106–109.
[197] For a full discussion of Moscheles' performances of Bach's music, as well as his membership in the Bach Gesellschaft of Leipzig, see Kroll, *Ignaz Moscheles*, pp. 263–274.
[198] Cited in F. G. E[dwards],"Bach's Music in England," p. 725.
[199] *The Atlas*, May 15, 1836, vol. XI, no. 522, p. 311.

Moscheles added – parts "for one Flute, two Clarinets, two Bassoons, and two Corni" – and why: "I mainly intended this wind-accompaniment to take the same position in the Concerto which is taken by the organ in the performance of a Mass."[200] Moscheles would also occasionally substitute movements from one Bach work to another, as he did for a performance of the *Triple Concerto in D Minor* on June 1, 1844.[201]

As the nineteenth century neared its midpoint, William Sterndale Bennett (1816–1875) began to make important contributions to the reception and acceptance of the music of J. S. Bach in Britain. Like Moscheles, Bennett was also inspired by Mendelssohn in his love of Bach, particularly after his visit to Leipzig in 1842.[202] The following year, Bennett started a series in London similar to Mendelssohn's, his "Classical Pianoforte Music," in which he performed a wide range of repertoire, including the first movement of Bach's D-minor concerto on June 16, 1847.[203] A concert on March 21, 1854, featured (as listed on the program) Bach's "Grand Fuga, A minor," "Duo (from Mass in B minor)," and the "Duett, Pianoforte and Violin, in E major" (i.e., the *Sonata for Violin and Harpsichord in E Major*, BWV 1016).[204] Critical reception to this series, however, was mixed and Bennett's chamber music concerts came to an end in 1856, when he became conductor of the Philharmonic Society. Bennett also launched a Bach Society in October 1849.[205] The works that he programmed or performed for the Society included solo keyboard music by Bach, such as selections from *The Well-Tempered Clavier*, the *Overture in the*

---

[200] Felix Moscheles, ed., *Letters of Felix Mendelssohn to Ignaz and Charlotte Moscheles*, pp. 152–153. Nevertheless, Moscheles admits: "I naturally hesitated . . . the worst that can be said of me is that I am but a poor imitator."

[201] See *AMZ*, June 3, 1844, no. 3, cols. 454–456, cited in Grossmann-Vendrey, *Felix Mendelssohn Bartholdy und die Musik der Vergangenheit*, p. 137.

[202] For information about Sterndale Bennett's visit to Leipzig in 1842 and the influence of Mendelssohn (and also Ferdinand David and the *Gewandhaus* concerts) on his interest in and activities on behalf of Bach's music, see Isabel Parrott, "William Sterndale Bennett and the Bach Revival in Nineteenth-Century England," in Rachel Cowgill and Julian Rushton, *Europe, Empire, and Spectacle in Nineteenth-Century British Music* (Aldershot: Ashgate, 2006), pp. 29–43.

[203] Kroll, *Ignaz Moscheles*, p. 303, citing Therese Ellsworth, "The Piano Concerto in London Concert Life between 1801 and 1850," Ph.D. diss., University of Cincinnati, 1991, pp. 148–149. See also Parrott, "William Sterndale Bennett and the Bach Revival in Nineteenth-Century England," pp. 31–32.

[204] See Parrott, "William Sterndale Bennett and the Bach Revival in Nineteenth-Century England," p. 31. A full list of works performed on this series can be found in Appendix 2.1A, p. 40.

[205] See Parrott, "William Sterndale Bennett and the Bach Revival in Nineteenth-Century England," pp. 34–35, and passim. See also Großmann-Vendrey, *Felix Mendelssohn Bartholdy und die Musik der Vergangenheit*, p. 199.

French Style in B minor, the *English Suite* no. 3 in G minor, violin and keyboard sonatas, and a variety of concerti and vocal works.[206]

J. S. Bach after 1850

The pianists mentioned in the sections on Scarlatti and Handel, such as Ernst Pauer, Anton Rubinstein, and Florence May, who were involved in "historical" recitals also included works by J. S. Bach on their programs. Pauer's program of 1867 featured J. S. Bach's "Italian Concerto," a choice that did not seem to please the reviewer, who wrote: "we cannot but think that a fairer specimen of the old Bach might have been chosen than his 'Italian Concerto,' in which Bach does not appear like Bach at all."[207] According to Hipkins, Pauer played "one of Bach's sonatas for piano and viol di gamba" in a concert at the Hanover Square Rooms on June 1869.[208] A safe assumption is that the solo string instrument was a cello rather than an actual viola da gamba. Hipkins himself performed the "Fantasia Cromatica" of Bach on "a good German clavichord," adding in the conclusion to his paper: "I will only further remark that the peculiar tone of the clavichord requires from the audience some concentration of the sense of hearing; after the first few bars all becomes clear."[209]

Julius Benedict, Ferdinand Hiller, and Arabella Goddard played the now ubiquitous triple concerto in D minor of Bach (BWV 1063?) in 1853. According to *The Musical World*, they even used Moscheles' version "in which the finale from another concerto in C is transposed to D, and substituted for the original last movement," the journal noting: "Severe Bachists might object to this, but the effect obtained certainly atones for the liberty taken with the great old contrapuntist." Remembering Mendelssohn's performance of 1844, the reviewer tells us that "each player introduced a cadenza at the point d'orgue in the first movement, that of M. Hiller being a masterly improvisation in a style that few pianists of the present era could approach."[210] A review of yet another performance of Bach's "triple concerto," this in 1867 by Clara Schumann, Arabella Goddard, and Charles Hall, refers to Moscheles' version, in which he had replaced the last movement with another, as mentioned

---

[206] For a full list of works by Bach performed in the Bach Society concerts, see Parrott, "William Sterndale Bennett and the Bach Revival in Nineteenth-Century England," Appendix 2.1B, pp. 41–42.

[207] *The Musical World*, December 21, 1867 (45:51), p. 866, and Kroll, *Ignaz Moscheles*, p. 304.

[208] See Holman, *Life after Death*, pp. 319 and 320, fn. 97.

[209] A. J. Hipkins, *The Old Clavier or Keyboard Instruments*, p. 145.

[210] See Kroll, *Ignaz Moscheles*, pp. 303, citing *The Musical World*, June 25, 1853 (31:26), p. 40.

previously; but by this time the journal had come to the conclusion that the use of Bach's original last movement was preferable.[211]

Bennett continued to promote and perform Bach's music. For example, during one of his chamber concerts in 1854, he played the piano part written by Mendelssohn to accompany Henry Vieuxtemps' performance of Bach's *Chaconne for Solo Violin* (BWV 1004), the *Musical World* reviewer commenting that a "modest but masterly pianoforte part, added by Mendelssohn, was played by Mr. Bennett to admiration, and the whole performance was perhaps the greatest treat of the concert."[212] His most noteworthy accomplishments as a Bach advocate in Britain after 1850 were the first performances in England of the *St. Matthew Passion*. The initial concert took place on April 6, 1854; subsequent complete performances were given on November 28, 1854, March 23, 1858, and May 24, 1862, and excerpts were presented on June 21, 1859, and July 24, 1860.[213] He had less success convincing the Royal Philharmonic Society to program pieces by Bach, although he was able to perform Bach's *Orchestral Suite in D Major* (BWV 1068) on May 18, 1857, the same piece conducted by Mendelssohn more than a decade earlier, on June 24, 1844.[214]

Turning to the Bach repertoire of the Philharmonic itself, it is no surprise that it got off to a late start programming his works. In fact, the first program featuring a work by Bach was that conducted by Mendelssohn in 1844, and an examination of Appendix 4 reveals that between 1844 and 1890, Bach's music appeared on only twenty-six concerts, far fewer than those of Handel during the nineteenth century, going all the way to 1895. The repertoire, moreover, consisted mostly of individual movements from instrumental works, such as Bach's unaccompanied violin sonatas or partitas, played by noted soloists, including Joseph Joachim and Eugène Ysaÿe; the "Fantasie Chromatique et Fugue" played by Hans von Bülow on April 28, 1873; or even an organ work performed by Saint-Saëns (July 2, 1879). Performances of Bach's vocal music by the Philharmonic were quite rare and consisted of excerpts, such as an aria from the "Agnus Dei" of the *Mass in B Minor* (May 22, 1878) or the aria "Erbarme Dich" from the *St. Matthew Passion* on June 30, 1880. The only complete instrumental (i.e., orchestral) works

[211] See Kroll, *Ignaz Moscheles*, pp. 303–304, citing *The Musical World*, April 13, 1867 (45:15), p. 233.

[212] The *Musical World*, 27 (July 8, 1854), p. 457, cited in Parrott, "William Sterndale Bennett and the Bach Revival in Nineteenth-Century England," p. 38. Mendelssohn's arrangement of the Chaconne was published by Ewer & Co. in London shortly after his death in 1847.

[213] See Parrott, "William Sterndale Bennett and the Bach Revival in Nineteenth-Century England," pp. 35–38 and 41–42; and R. Sterndale Bennett, "Three Abridged Versions of Bach's St. Matthew Passion," in Music & Letters, October 1956, vol. 37, no. 4, pp. 336–339.

[214] For information about this concert and the other works of Bach that Bennett programmed at the Philharmonic, see Parrott, "William Sterndale Bennett and the Bach Revival in Nineteenth-Century England," p. 33.

performed by the Royal Philharmonic over this period were the *Suite in D Major* (BWV 1068) in 1844 and 1857, as mentioned previously, which seems to have been repeated on March 11, 1867, and February 6, 1879; and a "Concerto for Strings in G" on June 24, 1872, this presumably referring to the *Brandenburg Concerto* No. 3 (BWV 1048), since this work is in G major and scored only for strings. Notably, the program listing for this concert proudly announces that this was the "First time of performance in England."

Epilogue

The fact that such an important and attractive work as a *Brandenburg Concerto* would have to wait until 1872 for its first major performance in Britain serves as eloquent testimony to some of the obstacles that the music of J. S. Bach faced in becoming accepted and better known during this period. The works of D. Scarlatti, and to a lesser extent Handel, faced their own set of problems and limitations, but all flourished, unexpectedly at times, thanks to the tireless efforts of innumerable musicians, academics, scholars, critics, religious leaders, politicians, members of the aristocracy, and the royal family, not to mention the public itself. Granted, in each case there were hurdles, misconceptions, passions, and prejudices that shaped the unique and sometimes idiosyncratic ways in which this music was performed, edited, and presented – from Avison's transformations of Scarlatti sonatas into concerti grossi, to the massive spectacle of the Handel commemorations or Moscheles' reorchestration of Bach's *Concerto for Harpsichord in D Minor* (BWV 1052) – but the fascinating history of their reception reminds us that we are still discovering how to interpret the music of these three great masters today. By taking into full account the extraordinary accomplishments made on their behalf between 1750 and 1850, we not only have the opportunity to hear Bach, Handel, and Scarlatti through the ears of the remarkable amateur and professional musicians of that era, but we can also gain insights into the complex and multifaceted ways in which any society – including our own – reimagines the music of the past.

Appendix 1

Performances of the Music of Handel at the Royal Philharmonic[215]

1818

March 9   Scena, "Ombre Sortite" (from the Opera of "Teseo")
                 Mr. Braham

1819

March 15   Duetto, "As steals the morn" (Il Moderato)
                 Miss Stephens and Mr. Braham
March 29   Aria "Dove sei" (Rodelinda)
                 Mrs. Salmon
June 7   Song, "From mighty Kings" (Judas Maccabaeus)
                 Mrs. Salmon

1820

April 24   Recit. and Air "From mighty Kings" (Judas Maccabeus)
                 [no singer listed]
May 8   Recit. and Air, "Deeper and deeper stil [sic]!"
                 Mr. Braham
                 Scena, "Berenice ove [sic] sei"
                 Mr. Braham

1821

May 28   Recit. and Air "From mighty Kings" (Judas Maccabaeus)
                 Mrs. Salmon

1822

April 29   Song, "Oft on a plat" (L'Allegro ed il Pensieroso)
                 Mr. Vaughan

---

[215] As listed in "The Philharmonic Society, Programs From Its Formation, March 8th, 1813 To The Last Concert Of The Present Season, June 17th," in *The Musical Courier*, June 25, 1896, pp. 715–758. All formatting is kept as close as possible to that of the original source.

1824

February 23	Trio, "The flocks shall leave the mountains" (Acis and Galatea) Madame Caradori, Mr. Vaughan, and Mr. Welsh
March 8	Recit. and Song, "From Mighty Kings" (Judas Maccabaeus) Mrs. Salmon
March 22	Song, "Heart, the seat of soft delight" (Acis and Galatea) Miss Stephens
April 5	Recit. and Air, "If guiltless blood" (Susanna) Mrs. Salmon
May 24	Duetto, As steals the Morn" (Il Moderato) Mrs. Salmon and Mr. Vaughan

1825

March 7	Trio, "The docks [sic] shall leave the mountains" Miss Stephens, Mr. Sapio, and Mr. Phillips (Acis and Galatea)
March 21	Song, Mr. Vaughan, "Why does the God of Israel sleep" (Samson)
April 11	Recit. and Air, "Deeper and deeper still" Mr. Sapio (Jephtha)

1826

June 12	Aria, Mr. Phillips, "Lascia amor"

1827

March 5	Recit. and Air, "Oh! ruddier than the cherry," and Trio, "The flocks shall leave," Miss Stephens, Mr. Sapio, and Signor Zuchelli (Acis and Galatea)
May 21	Recit. and Aria, Mr. Braham, "Deeper and deeper still" (Jephtha)

1828

June 9	Song, Mr. Phillips, "Revenge! Timotheus cries" (Alexander's Feast)

1829

May 11	Recitative, Mr. Phillips, "For behold." Song, "The people that walked" (The Messiah) with Mozart's accompaniments
May 25	Song, Miss Paton, "If guiltless blood" (Susanna)

1832

March 26   Aria, Mrs. Wood, "From mighty Kings" (Judas Maccabaeus)

1833

February 25   Aria, "Lascia amor"
                Mr. Phillips
March 11   Recit. ed Aria, "Morirò! ma vendicata" (Teseo)
                Miss Mason

1839

March 4   Song, "Revenge, Timotheus cries" (Alexander's Feast},
            Mr. Phillips

1841

May 17   Recit. ed Aria, Signor F. Lab'ache, "Ovoi [sic] dell' Erebo"
June 14   Air. Mr. Phillips, "Pour forth no more" (Jephtha)

1845

July 7   Aria, "Nasce al bosco" Staudigi (AEtius)

1848

June 12   Recit., "Armida dispietata"; Aria, "Lascia ch' io pianga"
           (Armida), Madame Pauline Viardot (with additional accompaniments by Meyerbeer)

1849

June 11   Aria, "Lascia amor" (Orlando)
           Mr. H. Phillips

1850

March 4   Recit., "Cease, O cease"; Trio, "The flocks shall leave the mountains"
           (Acis and Galatea),
           Miss Louisa Pyne, Mr. Benson, and Mr. Machin

1851

March 10   Aria, "Amor nel mio penar" (Flavio),
            Miss Dolby

1852

May 17   Aria, "Mis [sic] ben recordati [sic],"
          Miss Williams (*Poro*)
May 31   Recit., "Ma, che insolita luce"; Aria, "O voi dell Erebo" (La
          Risurrezione).
          Herr Staudigl
June 28   Recit., "Me. when the sun"; Aria, "Hide me from the day's garish
          eye" (L'Allegro ed il Pensieroso),
          Madame Clara Novello

1853

May 16   Overture, "Esther"
June 13   Recit., "Armida dispietata"; Aria, "Lascia ch'io pianga,"
          Madame Viardot (Armida)
July 4   Aria, "Return, O God of Hosts," Madame Viardot (Samson)

1855

May 28   Recit.., "I rage!" Song, "O ruddier than the cherry (Acie and Galatea)
          Herr Formes

1861

March 18   "Dead March in Saul"

1864

May 2   Aria, "Lascia Amor,"
          Mr. Weiss (Rinaldo)
June 27   Aria, "Lascia ch'io pianga,"
          Miss Louisa Pyne (Rinnaldo) [sic]

1868

June 8   Air and Variations from the Suite de Pièces in D minor.
          M. Antoine Rubinstein
July 17   Recit. ed Aria, "O voi dell'Erebo,"
          Mr. Santley (La Resurrezione)

1870

March 16   Song, "Love sounds the Alarm" (Acis & Galatea)
            Mr. Vernon Rigby

1871

May 8   Concerto grosso in G minor

1872

April 15   Concerto with Hautboy
             Oboe Solo, Mr. A. Lavigne
             Aria, "Mis [sic] bel tesoro" (Alcina)
             Mdlle. Anna Regan
             Scored for the Orchestra by Robert Franz
May 27   Song, "Revenge, Timotheus Cries" (*Alexander's Feast*)
             Mr. Santley

1874

March 25   Concerto Grosso, No. 11, in A
May 18   Aria, "Nasce al bosco" (*Ezio*)
             Mr. Santley

1875

May 10   Aria "Cangio d'aspetto"
             Miss Enriquez

1876

June 26   Aria, "Lascia ch'io pianga"
             Madame Bodda-Pyne (late Miss Louisa Pyne)
             (Her first appearance for five years)
July 10   Aria, "From mighty Kings" (Judas Maccabeus)
             Miss Emma Beasley

1877

February 22 Air, "Where'er you walk" (*Semele*)
             Mr. W. H. Cummings
March 8   Air, "Revenge: Timotheus cries"
             Herr Henschel
April 16   Recit. and {"Oh! didst thou know the pains"}
             Air ... {"As when the dove"} (Acis and Galatea)
             Mdlle. Thekla Friedländer

June 11	Recit. And Aria, "Lo! here my love," "Love in her eyes" (Acis and Galatea)
	Mr. Edward Lloyd
July 9	Song, "Heart, the seat of soft delight" (Acis and Galatea)
	Miss Catherine Penna

1878

March 14	Recit. ed [sic] Aria,"O voi dell' Erebo" (La Resurrezione)
	Mr. Santley
May 1	Air, "Sweet Bird" (L'Allegro ed il Pensieroso)
	Mdlle. Riego (from Theatre Royal, Stockholm)
	Flute Obbligato, Mr. Svendsen
June 12	Aria, "Mio caro bene" (Rodelinda)
	Miss Emma C. Thursby
July 3	Recit. and Air "Deeper and deeper still"
	"Waft her angels"
	Mr. Barton McGuckin

1879

April 30	Recit. and Air, "E pur cosi," "Piangerò" (Giulio Cesare)
	Miss Lillian Bailey (her first appearance)
	Duo, "Caro!" "Bella" (Giulio Cesare)
	Miss Bailey and Herr Henschel

1880

April 28	Recit. and Aria, "Lusinghe piu care" (Alessandro)
	Miss Lillian Bailey
June 9	Recit. and Air, "Ye Sacred Priests," "Farewell ye limpid springs"
	(Jephtha)
	Miss Mary Davies

1881

| February 24 | Aria, "Cangio d'aspetto" (Admeto) |
| | Madame Enriquez |

1884

| May 7 | Aria, "Revenge, Timotheus Cries" (Alexander's Feast) |
| | Mr. Santley |

1885

February 26	Aria (L'Allegro ed il Pensieroso), "Sweet Bird"
	Mdlle. Elly Warnots
	Flute Obligato, Mr. Olaf Svendsen
March 12	Overture, "The Occasional Oratorio"
May 20	Recit. ed Aria, "Sorge infausta una procella" (Orlando)
	Mr. Santley

1887

March 24	Air, "Let the Bright Seraphim" (Samson)
	Mdlle. Noridca
	(Her first appearance at these concerts)
	Trumpet,
	M. W. Ellis

1889

April 11	Songs (a) "Shall I in Mamre's fertile plain" (Joshua)
	(b) "Arise, y subterranean winds" (music to "The Tempest")
	Mr. W. H. Bereton (his first appearance at these concerts)
June 22	Air, "Return, oh! God of Hosts" (Samson),
	Fräulein Hermine Spies (her first appearance at these concerts)

1890

April 24	Aria, "Chi vive amante,"
	Miss Marian McKenzie (her first appearance at these concerts)
	(Poro)

1894

June 21	Aria, "Ombra mai fù" (Serse)
	Madame Amy Sherwin

1895

May 30	Recit. and Air from "Alessandro"
	Mrs. Henschel

Appendix 2

Performances of the Keyboard Music of Handel by Ignaz Moscheles

Suite for Harpsichord No. 1 in A major, Allemande and Gigue, HMV 426

Suite for Harpsichord No. 2 in F major, Allegro I and *II*, HMV 427

Suite for Harpsichord No. 3 in D minor, Prelude, Allegro, Air and Variations, HMV 428

Suite for Harpsichord No. 4 in E minor, Allegro, Allemande, Gigue, HMV 429

Suite for Harpsichord No. 5 in E major, Air and Variations ("The Harmonious Blacksmith"), HMV 430

Suite for Harpsichord No. 7 in G minor, Overture, Allegro, Gigue, Passacaille, HMV 432

As listed in programs

"Variations ("The Harmonious Blacksmith")" = *Air and Variations* from *Suite for Harpsichord No. 5 in E major*, HMV 430

"Allemande and a Gigue from the Suite premiere pour le Clavecin to which MR. MOSCHELES added the fugue in F major from the second suite, and the notable fugue in E minor."

"*Allemande* and a *Gigue* from the *Suite premiere pour le Clavecin* = *Allemande and Gigue, Suite for Harpsichord No. 1 in A major*, HMV 426

"Fugue in F major" = *Allegro II, Suite for Harpsichord No. 2 in F major*, HMV 427

"Fugue in E minor" = *Allegro, Suite for Harpsichord No. 4 in E minor*, HMV 429

"Aria in D minor, and Fugue in E minor, from Handel's Suites"

"Aria in D minor" = *Air* from *Suite for Harpsichord No. 3 in D minor*, HMV 428

"Fugue in E minor" = *Allegro, Suite for Harpsichord No. 4 in E minor*, HMV 429

"Courante, Fugue and Gigue, in G minor" = *Allegro and Gigue, Suite for Harpsichord no. 7 in G minor*, HMV 432. There is no "fugue" in this suite

"SUITE DE PIECES, (written for the Clavecin) Sarabande with Variations— Fugue in E minor— Allemande—Jigg." = *Allemande* and *Gigue, Suite for Harpsichord No. 4 in E minor*, HMV 429

Sarabande with Variations = unidentifiable

"Prelude and Fugue in E minor, Allemande and Fugue in F major"

"Prelude and Fugue in E minor" = *Allegro, Suite for Harpsichord No. 4 in E minor*, HMV 429. "Fugue" unidentifiable

"Allemande and Fugue in F major" = *Allegro I* and *Allegro II, Suite for Harpsichord No. 2 in F major*, HMV 427

"Prelude and Fugue in D minor, Air and Variations (from the Suites des Pieces)"

"Prelude and Fugue in D minor" = *Prelude* and *Allegro, Suite for Harpsichord No. 3 in D minor*, HMV 428

"Air and Variations, (from the Suites des Pieces)" = *Air* and *Variations, Suite for Harpsichord No. 3 in D minor*, HMV 428

Appendix 3

Keyboard, Chamber, and Vocal Music of Johann Sebastian Bach Performed by Ignaz Moscheles Solo Keyboard

Chromatic Fantasy and Fugue (BWV 903)
The Well-Tempered Clavier, Books I and II (unspecified):

"Three Preludes and Fugues (C-sharp major, C-sharp minor, D major)"
"Three Preludes & Fugues, (D major, F sharp minor, and A flat major)"
"Three Preludes and Fugues, B flat major, G sharp minor, and B major)"
"Prelude and Fugue (C major,) Prelude and Fugue (E major)"
"Preludes in D major, F sharp major, and A flat major, (all to be found in the third and fourth books of WESLEY and HORN'S edition)" (i.e., Book II)

Ricercare (either 3-part or 6-part) from *Musical Offering* (BWV 1079)
"*Toccata et fugue*, in E major" (i.e., probably *Toccata in E minor*, BWV 914)
"Two Preludes and Fugues (E minor and F major, as written for the organ)," Probably *Prelude and Fugue in E minor*, BWV 533 or 548, and *Prelude and Fugue in F major*, BWV 556
"Preludes and Fugues in E Minor and D major, from Bach's Organ Compositions,"
Prelude and Fugue in D major, (probably BWV 532?)

Concertos

Concerto for Three Harpsichords in D Minor, BWV 1063
Concerto for Harpsichord in D minor, BWV 1052
Concerto for Harpsichord in G minor, BWV 1058
Concerto for Harpsichord in D Major, BWV 1054
Triple Concerto for Violin, Flute, and Harpsichord in A minor, BWV 1044
Concerto for Harpsichord and Two Recorders in F major, BWV 1057
"Concerto for pianoforte, two flutes, and double quartet" and "(Unpublished) MS. Concerto with two Obligato Flutes and Quartett Accompaniments" (probably Bach's arrangement of the *Brandenburg Concerto No. 4 in G major*, BWV 1049)

Chamber Music

Sonata for Violin and Harpsichord in E major, BWV 1016
"SONATA, C major, pianoforte and violin" (i.e., possibly *C minor*, BWV 1017,
   since the only violin sonata in C major is the *Sonata for Unaccompanied
   Violin*, BWV 1055)
Trio Sonata, Musical Offering (BWV 1079)

Vocal Music

"Sacred Song, Dost thou despise the riches of his mercy, Mr. Stretton (from the
   selection of Church Music), first time of performance in this country."
Probably the bass aria, "Verachtest du den Reichtum seiner Gnade," from the
   cantata *Herr Deine Augen sehen nach dem Glauben*, BWV 102

Unidentifiable

"Concerto for Harpsichord in C minor" (BWV 981 or BWV 1062 for two
   harpsichords?)

Appendix 4

Performance of the Music of J.S. Bach at the Royal Philharmonic Society, 1844–1890[216]

1844

| June 24 | Overture and Suite (first time of performance in this country) |

1857

| May 18 | Overture (ou Suite), in D major |

1858

| May 24 | Sonata Violin, Herr Joachim |

1859

| May 2 | Solo, Violo [sic], "Chaconne" [Joachim] |
| June 13 | Aria, "My heart, with pious faith rejoice," Madame Clara Novello (with Violoncello Obligato, Mr. Lucas) |

1862

March 10	Sarabande, Double Bourée, *Double*, Violin, Herr Joachim
March 24	Prelude and Fugue alla Tarantella, Miss Arabella Godard
April 7	Andante Fuga, Violin Solo, Herr Joachim

1864

| May 16 | Prelude and Fugue alla Tarantella, Pianoforte, Madame Arabella Goddard |

---

[216] As listed in "The Philharmonic Society, Programs From Its Formation, March 8th, 1813 To The Last Concert Of The Present Season, June 17th," in *The Musical Courier*, June 25, 1896, pp. 715–758. All formatting is kept as close as possible to that of the original source.

May 30   Solos, Violin, Herr Joachim
              Prelude

1867

March 25   Overture or Suite in D

1869

March 10   Solos for Violin (a), Abendlied, Schumann; (b), Loure, Allegro in E;
              Violin, Herr Joachim

1872

May 13   Toccata Pedalier, Grand Pianoforte,
              Mons. E. M. Delaborde
June 24   Concerto for Strings in G (First time of performance in England)

1873

April 28   Fantasie Chromatique et Fugue en Re Mineur,
              Pianoforte, Dr. Hans von Bulow

1874

June 29   Toccata (arranged by Tausig),
              Pianoforte, Madame Essipoff

1876

May 15   Suite in B minor
              Flute obligato, Mr. Olaf Svendsen

1878

February 14   Andante and Finale from Sonata in C (unaccompanied) Violin,
              Herr Joachim
May 22   Aria, "Agnus Dei" (Mass in B minor)
              Madame Patey

1879

February 6   Suite in D
February 20   Sarabande and Bouree from Suite in B minor (unaccompanied
              Violin),
              Herr Joachim

July 2   *Prelude & Fugue in A minor,*
                Organ, M. Saint-Saens

1880

March 18   Sarabande, Double, Bourree, Double from Suite in B minor for
                Violin alone
                Herr Joachim
June 30   Aria, "Erbarme Dich" (St. Matthew Passion)
                Madame Antoinette Sterling
                Violin Obligato, Herr L. Straus

1883

March 1   Suite in D
April 25   Prelude in A,
                Madame Sophie Menter

1887

April 21   Solo, Piano pedalier, "Toccata in F,"
                Madame Lucie Palicot

1889

March 14   Fantasia in C minor,
                Fraulein [sic] Geisler.

1890

March 13   Air, "Je brave les jaloux" (Le défi de Phébus et de Pan),
                Mr. E. Blauwaert (his first appearance at these concerts)
March 27   Violin Solo, *Prelude and Gavotte*, in E [Major],
                M. Ysaye

Bibliography

Ackermann, Peter, Jacobshagen, Arnold, Scoccimarro, Roberto, Steinbeck, Wolfram, and Schnapper, Laure. *Ferdinand Hiller: Komponist, Interpret, Musikvermittler*. Berlin: Merseburger, 2014.

Avison, Charles. *An Essay on Musical Expression . . . The Second Edition, with Alterations and Large Additions*. London: C. Davis, 1753. Facsimile edition, New York: Broude Brothers, 1967.

Boyd, Malcolm. *Domenico Scarlatti – Master of Music*. New York: Schirmer Books, 1986.

Bruce, Robert J. and Johnstone, H. Diack. "A Catalogue of the Truly Valuable and Curious Library of Music in the Possession of Dr. William Boyce (1779)." *Royal Music Association Research Chronicle*, no. 43 (2010), pp. 111–171.

Burney, Charles. *A General History of Music from the Earliest Ages to the Present Period (1789)*, 2 vols., edited by Frank Mercer. New York: Dover Publications, 1957.

Carew, Derek. *The Mechanical Muse: The Pianos, Pianism and Piano Music, c. 1760–1850*. Aldershot: Ashgate, 2007.

Carnelly, John. *George Smart and 19th-Century London Concert Life*. Woodbridge: The Boydell Press, 2015.

Coke, David and Borg, Alan. *Vauxhall Gardens: A History*. New Haven: Yale University Press, 2011.

Cook, Nicholas and Everist, Mark, eds. *Rethinking Music*. Oxford: Oxford University Press, 1999.

Cowgill, Rachel and Rushton, Julian, eds. *Europe, Empire, and Spectacle in Nineteenth-Century British Music*. Aldershot: Ashgate, 2006.

Crotch, William. *Elements of Musical Composition*. London: Longman, Hurst, Rees, Orme, & Brown, 1812.

    Specimens on Various Styles of Music Referred to in a Course of Lectures, Read at Oxford and London, and Adapted to Keyed Instruments. London: R. Birchall, ca. 1815.

    Substance of Several Courses of Lectures on Music, Read in the University of Oxford and in the Metropolis. London: Longman, Rees, Orme, Brown, and Green, 1831.

Cypess, Rebecca and Sinkoff, Nancy, eds. *Sara Levy's World: Gender, Judaism, and the Bach Tradition in Enlightenment Berlin*. Rochester: University of Rochester Press, 2018.

Davison, Carol Margaret. *Gothic Literature, 1764–1824*. Cardiff: University of Wales Press, 2009.

Daw, Stephen. "Muzio Clementi as an Original Advocate, Collector and Performer, in Particular of J. S. Bach and D. Scarlatti." In *Bach, Handel, Scarlatti Tercentenary Essays*, edited by Peter Williams. Cambridge: Cambridge University Press, 1985, pp. 61–74.

Drummond, Pippa. *The Provincial Music Festival in England, 1784–1914*. Surrey: Ashgate, 2011.

Eatcock, Colin Timothy. *Mendelssohn and Victorian England*. Surrey: Ashgate, 2009.

Edwards, Frederick George. "Bach's Music in England." *The Musical Times and Singing Class Circular*, vol. 37, no. 645 (Nov. 1, 1896), pp. 722–726.

Eggington, Tim. *The Advancement of Music in Enlightenment England; Benjamin Cooke and the Academy of Ancient Music*. Woodbridge: The Boydell Press, 2014.

Ellis, Katherine. *Interpreting the Musical Past*. Oxford: Oxford University Press, 2008.

Ellsworth, Therese and Wollenberg, Susan. *The Piano in Nineteenth-Century British Culture: Instruments, Performers and Repertoire*. London: Routledge, 2007.

Fétis, François-Joseph and Moscheles, Ignaz. *Méthode des Méthodes*. Paris: Maurice Schlesinger, 1840. Facsimile edition, Minkoff Reprint, Geneva, 1973.

Gamer, Michael. *Romanticism and the Gothic: Genre, Reception, and Canon Formation*. Cambridge: Cambridge University Press, 2004.

Germann, George. *Gothic Revival in Europe and Britain: Sources, Influences and Ideas*. London: Lund Humphries with the Architectural Association, 1972.

Grimes, Nicole and Mace, Angela R. *Mendelssohn Perspectives*. Surrey: Ashgate, 2012.

Großmann-Vendrey, Susanna. *Felix Mendelssohn Bartholdy und die Musik der Vergangenheit*. Regensburg: Gustav Bosse Verlag, 1969.

Haskell, Harry. *The Early Music Revival: A History*. London: Thames & Hudson, 1988.

Hawkins, Sir John. A *General History of the Science and Practice of Music*. London: T. Payne and Son, 1776.

Heller, Wendy. *Music in the Baroque*. New York: W. W. Norton, 2013.

Hipkins, Alfred James. "The Old Clavier or Keyboard Instruments; Their Use by Composers, and Technique." *Proceedings of the Musical Association, 12th Sess. (1885–1886)*, pp. 139–148.

Holman, Peter. *Life after Death: The Viola da Gamba in Britain from Purcell to Dolmetsch*. Woodbridge: The Boydell Press, 2010.

"The Conductor at the Organ, or How Choral and Orchestral Music Was Directed in Georgian England." In *Music and Performance Culture in Nineteenth-Century Britain: Essays in Honour of Nicholas Temperley*, edited by Bennett Zon. Farnham: Ashgate, 2012, pp. 243–261.

Before the Baton: Musical Direction and Conducting in Stuart and Georgian Britain. Woodbridge: The Boydell Press, 2020.

Hyatt King, Alexander. "English Royal Music-Lovers and Their Library, 1600–1900." *The Musical Times*, vol. 99, no. 1384 (Jun. 1958), pp. 311–313.

Some British Collectors of Music c.1600–1960. Cambridge: Cambridge University Press, 1963.

Irving, Howard. *Ancients and Moderns: William Crotch and the Development of Classical Music*. Aldershot: Ashgate, 1999.

Johnson, Claudia L. "'Giant HANDEL' and the Musical Sublime." *Eighteenth-Century Studies*, vol. 19, no. 4 (Summer 1996), pp. 515–533.

Kassler, Michael, ed. *The English Bach Awakening: Knowledge of J. S. Bach and His Music in England 1750–1830*. Aldershot: Ashgate, 2004.

Kassler, Michael and Olleson, Philip. *Samuel Wesley (1766–1837): A Source Book*. Aldershot: Ashgate, 2001.

Kirkpatrick, Ralph. *Domenico Scarlatti*. Princeton, NJ: Princeton University Press, 1983.

Kroll, Mark. *Johann Nepomuk Hummel: A Musician's Life and World*. Lanham, MD: Scarecrow Press, 2007.

Ignaz Moscheles and the Changing World of Musical Europe. Woodbridge: The Boydell Press, 2014.

"*Con Furia*: Charles Avison and the Scarlatti Sect in Eighteenth-Century England." In *The Early Keyboard Sonata in Italy and Beyond*, edited by Rohan H. Stewart-MacDonald. Turnhout: Brepols, 2016, pp. 252–277.

"Moscheles, Handel and the Performance and Reception of Old Music in Nineteenth-Century England." *Early Music Performer: Journal of the National Early Music Association*, no. 42 (2018), pp. 17–29.

Johann Nepomuk Hummel: A Complete Theoretical & Practical Course of Instructions on the Art of Playing the Piano Forte. London: T. Boosey, 1828. Facsimile of Part III of the Boston edition. Hillsdale, NY: Pendragon Press, 2019.

Lawson, Colin and Stowell, Robin. *The Historical Performance of Music*. Cambridge: Cambridge University Press, 1999.

Little, William A. *Mendelssohn and the Organ*. Oxford: Oxford University Press, 2010.

Lovell, Percy. "'Ancient' Music in Eighteenth-Century England." *Music & Letters*, vol. 60, no. 4 (Oct. 1979), pp. 401–415.

Marvin, Roberta Montemorra. "Handel's *Acis and Galatea*: A Victorian View." In *Europe, Empire, and Spectacle in Nineteenth-Century British Music*, edited by Rachel Cowgill and Julian Rushton. Aldershot: Ashgate, 2006, pp. 249–264.

McVeigh, Simon. "Italian Violinists in Eighteenth-Century London." In *The Eighteenth-Century Diaspora of Italian Music and Musicians*, edited by Reinhard Strohm. Turnhout: Brepols, 2001, pp. 139–176.

Concert Life in London from Mozart to Haydn. Cambridge: Cambridge University Press, 1993.

Moscheles, Felix. *Letters of Felix Mendelssohn to Ignaz and Charlotte Moscheles: Translated from the Originals in His Possession and Edited by Felix Moscheles*. Freeport, NY: Books for Libraries Press, 1970.

Moscheles, Ignatz. *Recent Music and Musicians, Edited by His Wife and Adapted from the Original German by A. D. Coleridge*. New York: Henry Holt and Company, 1873.

Newton, Richard. "The English Cult of Domenico Scarlatti." *Music & Letters*, vol. 20, no. 2 (Apr. 1939), pp. 138–156.

Olleson, Philip. *The Letters of Samuel Wesley: Professional and Social Correspondence, 1797–1837*. Oxford: Oxford University Press, 2001.

"Samuel Wesley and the Development of the Organ Pedals in England." In *Music and Performance Culture in Nineteenth-Century Britain: Essays in Honour of Nicholas Temperley*, edited by Bennett Zon. Surrey: Ashgate, 2012, pp. 283–297.

Olleson, Philip and Palmer, Fiona M. "Publishing Music from the Fitzwilliam Museum, Cambridge; the Work of Vincent Novello and Samuel Wesley in the 1820s." *Journal of the Royal Musical Association*, vol. 130, no. 1 (2005), pp. 38–73.

Parke, W. T. *Musical Memoirs; Comprising an Account of the General State of Music in England from the First Commemoration of Handel in 1784, to the Year 1830*. New York: Da Capo Press, 1970.

Parrott, Isabel. "William Sterndale Bennett and the Bach Revival in Nineteenth-Century England." In *Europe, Empire, and Spectacle in Nineteenth-Century British Music*, edited by Rachel Cowgill and Julian Rushton. Aldershot: Ashgate, 2006, pp. 29–43.

Plantinga, Leon. *Clementi: His Life and Music*. London: Oxford University Press, 1977.

Price, Uvedale. *An Essay on the Picturesque, as Compared with the Sublime and the Beautiful*, rev. ed. London: J. Robson, 1796–1798.

Rackwitz, Werner. "Ignaz Moscheles – sein Verhältnis zur Musik Georg Friedrich Händel." *Göttinger Händel-Beiträge*, vol. 13 (2012), pp. 219–243.

Rainbow, Bernarr. *Four Centuries of Teaching Manuals, 1518–1932*. Woodbridge: The Boydell Press, 1992.

Richards, Annette. *The Free Fantasia and the Musical Picturesque*. Cambridge: Cambridge University Press, 2001.

Ritterman, Janet and Weber, William. "Origins of the Piano Recital in England, 1830–1870." In *The Piano in Nineteenth-Century British Culture: Instruments, Performers and Repertoire*, edited by Therese Ellsworth and Susan Wollenberg. London: Routledge, 2007, pp. 171–192.

Robins, Brian. *The John Marsh Journals: The Life and Times of a Gentleman Composer (1752–1828)*. Stuyvesant, NY: The Pendragon Press, 1998.

Rosenblum, Sandra P. "New Introduction." In *Introduction to the Art of Playing on the Piano Forte by Muzio Clementi*. New York: Da Capo Press, 1974. Reprint of the 1st ed., 2nd issue, 1801, published by Clementi, Banger, Hyde, Collard & Davis, London.

Rowland, David. *The Cambridge Companion to the Piano*. Cambridge: Cambridge University Press, 1998.

Stephens, Norris Lynn. "Charles Avison: An Eighteenth-Century English Composer, Musician and Writer." Ph.D. diss., University of Pittsburgh, 1968.

Sterndale, Bennett R. "Three Abridged Versions of Bach's *St. Matthew Passion*." *Music & Letters*, October 1956, vol. 37, no. 4, pp. 336–339.

Stinson, Russell. *The Reception of Bach's Organ Works from Mendelssohn to Brahms*. Oxford: Oxford University Press, 2006.

Taylor, Ian. *Music in London and the Myth of Decline*. Cambridge: Cambridge University Press, 2010.

Temperley, Nicholas. "The Prince Consort, Champion of Music," *The Musical Times*, vol. 102, no. 1426 (Dec. 1961), pp. 762–764.

"London and the Piano, 1760–1860." *The Musical Times*, vol. 129, no. 1744 (Jun. 1988), pp.289–293.

"The Music of Dissent." In *Dissenting Praise: Religious Dissent and the Hymn in England and Wales*, edited by Isabel Rivers and David L.Wykes. Oxford: Oxford University Press, 2011, chapter 8. DOI: 10.1093/acprof: oso/9780199545247.001.0001.

Thistlethwaite, Nicholas and Webber, Geoffrey. *The Cambridge Companion to the Organ*. Cambridge: Cambridge University Press, 1998.

Todd, Larry. *Mendelssohn: A Life in Music*. Oxford: Oxford University Press, 2003.

Tomita, Yo. "'Most ingenious, most learned, and yet practicable work': The English Reception of Bach's *Well-Tempered Clavier* in the First Half of the Nineteenth Century Seen through the Editions Published in London." In *The Piano in Nineteenth-Century British Culture*, edited by Therese Ellsworth and Susan Wollenberg. London: Routledge, 2007, pp. 33–67.

Wangermée, Robert. "Les Premiers Concerts Historiques à Paris." *Mélanges Ernest Closson*. Brussels: Societé belge de musicologie, 1948, pp. 185–196.

François-Joseph Fétis: musicologue et compositeur. Bruxelles: Palais des Académies, 1951.

"Les techniques de la vituosité pianistique selon Fétis." *Revue belge de Musicologie*, vol. 26 (1972–1973), pp. 90–105.

Weber, William. *The Rise of Musical Classics in Eighteenth-Century England: A Study in Canon, Ritual, and Ideology*. Oxford: Clarendon Press, 1992.

Wollenberg, Susan. "Music in 18th-Century Oxford." *Proceedings of the Royal Musical Association*, vol. 108 (1981–1982), pp. 69–99.

Music at Oxford in the Eighteenth and Nineteenth Centuries. Oxford: Oxford University Press, 2001.

Acknowledgments

I wish to offer my thanks to my editor Simon Keefe for his invaluable support and advice in shepherding this Element to completion, and to Kate Brett of Cambridge University Press, whose encouragement and good ideas for this publication, as well as my *Cambridge Companion to the Harpsichord*, have always been welcome.

I am very grateful to Professor Wendy Heller, Professor Robert Marshall, and Dr. Valerie Walden for reading various versions of the Element. Their knowledge and expertise made it better in countless ways. I once again offer my gratitude to Professor Carol Lieberman, my wife and a violinist with whom I have shared a fifty-year performing career. She has read every word I have written, many times over. Her contributions have been invaluable and deeply appreciated.

Cambridge Elements ≡

Elements in Music and Musicians 1750–1850

Simon P. Keefe

University of Sheffield

Simon P. Keefe is James Rossiter Hoyle Chair of Music at the University of Sheffield. He is the author of four books on Mozart, including *Mozart in Vienna: the Final Decade* (Cambridge University Press, 2017) and *Mozart's Requiem: Reception, Work, Completion* (Cambridge University Press, 2012), which won the Marjorie Weston Emerson Award from the Mozart Society of America. He is also the editor of seven volumes for Cambridge University Press, including *Mozart Studies* and *Mozart Studies 2*. In 2005 he was elected a life member of the Academy for Mozart Research at the International Mozart Foundation in Salzburg.

About the Series

Music and Musicians, 1750–1850 explores musical culture in the late eighteenth and early nineteenth centuries through individual, cutting-edge studies (c. 30,000 words) that imaginatively re-think a period traditionally associated with high classicism and early romanticism. The series interrogates images and reputations, composers, instruments and performers, critical and aesthetic ideas, travel and migration, and music and social upheaval (including wars and conflicts), thereby demonstrating the cultural vibrancy of the period. Through discussion of musicians' interactions with one another and with non-musicians, real-world experiences in and outside music, evolving reputations, and little studied career contexts and environments, Music and Musicians, 1750–1850 works across the conventional "silos" of composer, genre, style, and place, as well as in many instances across the (notional) 1800 divide. All contributions appeal to a wide readership of scholars, students, practitioners and informed musical public.

Cambridge Elements $^{\equiv}$

Elements in Music and Musicians 1750–1850

Printed in the United States
by Baker & Taylor Publisher Services